THE REVIEW OF CONTEMPORARY FICTION

BACK ISSUES AVAILABLE

Back issues are still available for the following numbers of the
Review of Contemporary Fiction ($8 each unless otherwise noted):

Individuals receive a 10% discount on orders of one issue and a 20% di
of two or more issues. To place an order, use the form on the last pag

Dalkey Archive Press announces a **call**
for **submissions** to the

DALKEY ARCHIVE
SCHOLARLY SERIES

(expanding opportunities for
specialized scholarly research)

AREAS OF INTEREST:

- **monographs** on authors from throughout the
  world in the aesthetic tradition represented
  by Dalkey Archive Press's list

- **encyclopedic companions** to contemporary
  fiction from around the world

- **literary history** and **theory**

- **cultural studies**

- **collections of interviews**

- **aesthetics**

- **bibliographies** of contemporary novelists

For further details related to submission, please visit
www.dalkeyarchive.com/resources

DALKEY ARCHIVE PRESS

Spring 2007   Vol. XXVII, no. 1
ISSN: 0276-0045   ISBN-13: 978-1-56478-472-8

THE REVIEW OF CONTEMPORARY FICTION

Editor
JOHN O'BRIEN

Managing Editor
MARTIN RIKER

Associate Editor
IRVING MALIN

Book Review Editor
MICHAEL SQUEO

Editorial Assistant
GRETCHEN JOHNSON

Production & Design
LOUIS MORTON

Published at the University of Illinois at Urbana-Champaign.
No part of this periodical may be reproduced
without the permission of the publisher.

www.dalkeyarchive.com

The *Review of Contemporary Fiction* is published three times each year
(January, June, September).
ISSN 0276-0045.
Subscription prices are as follows:

Single volume (three issues):
Individuals: $17.00; foreign, add $3.50.
Institutions: $26.00; foreign, add $3.50.

This issue is partially supported by a grant from
the Illinois Arts Council, a state agency,
and the University of Illinois, Urbana-Champaign.

Indexed in *American Humanities Index, International Bibliography of
Periodical Literature, International Bibliography of Book
Reviews, MLA Bibliography,* and *Book Review Index.* Abstracted
in *Abstracts of English Studies.*

The *Review of Contemporary Fiction* is also available on 16mm
microfilm, 35mm microfilm, and 105mm microfiche from
University Microfilms International, 300 North Zeeb Road,
Ann Arbor, MI 48106-1346.

www.dalkeyarchive.com

Contents

A Short Introduction

This will be a short introduction, with a few asides.

1. Why this issue? Simply: selections from a number of Dalkey Archive books that reviewers did not respond well to when first published, or some of the reprints that the Press published because the critics also didn't get them when they first came out from other publishers years ago.

2. Why didn't the reviewers like them? We don't know. They either ignored them completely, or they announced, as if a public health warning, that the books "weren't"—to use a favorite phrase—"for everyone."

3. What did they mean? They meant that the books presented "difficulties." You will be able to judge for yourself here how difficult these books are.

4. Wherein lies the "difficulty"? The books challenge certain assumptions about what a novel is, unwelcome in many circles. Careers are built around certain ideas of what fiction is or should aspire to be. Such as? That there should be a "story"; that characters should be sympathetic; that fiction should teach us something or other, usually a lesson, a social or political lesson; that the author is trying to "say something" that will be of value as we return to our "real" lives, as though the experience of art is not part of our real lives; that art should be simply comforting (reaffirming all that we already know, about both art and the "real world") while at the same time allowing us to feel as though we are discovering these things for the first time; that fiction should be "easy," in the way that a PBS documentary is "easy," or a Garrison Keillor poem read each morning to hundreds of thousands of people: something simple, ennobling, a wise observation, a moving anecdote, etc.

5. And what would these same reviewers make of *Don Quixote*, *Tristram Shandy*, *Ulysses*, *The Sound and the Fury*, or *Remembrance of Things Past* if they were delivered to them today as new books? Too long, too difficult, self-indulgent, EXPERIMENTAL, not for everybody.

6. William Carlos Williams said almost a century ago that Americans (meaning the critics) will condemn anything "new." Indeed. And they go on condemning Williams himself to this day, but with a measure of respect, with a certain sense that they cannot appear to be Yahoos.

7. And yet, with growing frequency, the critics become bolder, self-righteous, arrogant, condescending. Once upon a time, even an Edmund Wilson would have to be measured by what he had to say about, for instance, Joyce. But now we have critics, ill read yet opinionated, who say what they want, apparently without an editor who knows any more than they do. One opinion as good as the next. No breadth of knowledge against which to judge the book before them except that it wasn't as inspiring as some recent novel from Scribner's that revealed something or other about something or other. Just read your Sunday book-review supplement (if you still have one in your local paper) to see what's said.

8. Or consider this: the word "elitist" is nasty in our culture, smacking of wealth, exclusiveness, arrogance. It's a word that has often been associated with Dalkey Archive. And it's a word that, when invoked, is greeted with mindless nods of many heads: elitist is bad, who can argue?

9. But what might "elitist" means as related to literature? It often means, simply, "excellence." And excellence in literature is something that crosses social and economic barriers. In this respect, literature is one of the few potentially democratic arenas left to us; great literature is available to everyone, or at least to anyone not too caught up in preconceptions about literary value as to miss the value of what's right in front of them.

10. Is it really available to everyone? Doesn't it require a graduate-level education? We would not have published these works if we thought so. In fact, the educated—or we'll say the "officially" educated—are just as likely to have problems with this type of writing, since it operates in traditions outside the ones they've been educated into. It would be hard for anyone to read a writer such as Vedrana Rudan, for example, or Gert Jonke, or any of the other writers included here, and not understand that their works stand in opposition to the narrow limits of our official education. A

constant questioning of the establishment, both the social establishment and the literary one—that is what reviewers are really talking about when they call this work "difficult."

11. Of course these are just our answers to these questions. The pieces collected here answer them in their own ways, and more adeptly than anything anyone is going to write about them. They are, when taken in their totality, remarkable expressions of what can be done in fiction when released from well-worn conventions. Readers are oftentimes placed in unfamiliar territory and must—to one degree or another—find their way around, a supreme compliment from an author to a reader. Readers do not create the text but, in some indefinable way, complete it. For some readers, this experience constitutes literature's greatest pleasure.

John O'Brien
Martin Riker

from

Teitlebaum's Window

Wallace Markfield

Then in June, 1932, on the second Saturday, a year exactly till
Teitlebaum would start in with his signs ("President Roosevelt
had a hundred days but you got only till this Monday to enjoy such
savings on our Farm Girl pot cheese"), not long after the Workmen's
Circle took out space in the *Coney Island Bulletin* urging total
membership to stay away from French wines and perfumes until
Léon Blum was restored to his parliament; also the same week
Luna Park finished off a lousy season with a nice fire; a day after
Ringelman, the Dentist, got his glasses broken by Mrs. Weigholtz
for proposing certain advanced oral-hygiene treatments; around
the time Harry the Fish Man's daughter, Fat Rosalie, gave away
her father's beautiful little Schaeffer pen for a Suchard, the semi-
sweet; not too long after Margoshes of the *Forvitz* ran this little
item at the foot of his column: "Which hotsy-totsy Mexican actress
should be called Amhoretz Del Rio for denying her Jewish blood?";
around the time Mrs. Faygelees kept calling and calling the *News*
to find out when Elinor Ames would be using her question ("Should
the son of a sick mother whose husband was put on a piecework
basis have to pay for the Gravesend Avenue line transfer of a girl
not from his faith?"); nine days since Block and Sully and Belle
Baker were on the Rudy Vallee show; this also happening to be the
day Gromajinski the Super, in a fit of drunken Polish rage, snipped
every radio aerial on the roof of 2094 Brighton Beach Avenue; while
Mrs. Aranow's Stanley was still telling the story of how he had
been hailed at Grand Central Station by this fellow in a racoon
coat and a straw skimmer; how this fellow finished off a whole hip
flask during the thirty-five cent ride; how he put three dimes and
five pennies into Stanley's palm; how Stanley had extended his
arm, saying "Mister, we work for tips" or "Mister, we depend on
tips"; how talking and talking of the cabbie's plight he kept this
arm extended; how this fellow had smashed at the arm with a
cruel-looking cane and said through his fat nose, "Godfrey Daniel,
if there's one thing I can't stand it's a one-armed cabdriver!"; while

Mary Mixup still had her share, and more than her share, from Bicep the Wrestler; even as Benny still could not get himself to drown his kittens; right after Smitty tried out for a job with Mr. Bailey;

Simon Sloan, all rosy and redolent of matzo and milk, waited till his father, whiffing and chuffing and grumbling away in some old argument, fell into a fuddled snooze. Then with both hands busy Simon came rolling over on top of his mother, going "Lemme lemme!"

"In case Cousin Phillie comes over tonight"—his mother took love-bites at his behind—"that's just in case, and he wants you should kiss him, remember you mustn't, you dassn't dassn't say to him, 'Go way vomithead!' "

"What he is," said Simon as he cupped and clutched.

"You should do a shake-hands with him, a 'How are you' and a 'What's new, Cousin Phillie,' " his mother droned drowsily, "and then you can say to him in a nice way, a not fresh way, 'The reason why I didn't kiss you, Cousin Phillie, is on account of I'm only only eight years old and they're not teaching yet in my 3B1 to be a two-face and you shouldn't expect it from me as I know the whole whole tragic story of what you and yours did to my Mommy, Malvena the Orphan, how you gave her a misleading, you begged and begged her she should come and work for you in Hartford, Connecticut, she wouldn't never never know again from a bad minute, sure she wouldn't know, how was she going to know, the first thing you did you took away from her her watch . . .' "

Simon crooned, softly crooned,

> *A my name is Aaron*
> *And my wife's name is Anna*
> *We come from Alabama*
> *And we sell . . . ALPS!*

"Without opening a big mouth you'll tell him also how he repaid your mommy . . ."

"*Pogrom*," Simon's father mumbled from his deepest sleep.

"That when she got so so sick and they wanted her to come and bring with her a urination specimen in a bottle you docked her three cents for the bottle."

"Heh heh," went Simon. He pointed and poked. "When they jiggle you know what they look like, Mommy? Heh? Heh, Mommy?"

"In a pleasant way you can mention he's still still throwing up how when your Mommy got married he took care of the liquor."

"Just just just like Betty Boop's eyes!" Simon exclaimed wonderingly.

"You can tell him, 'Cousin Phillie, I heard already how you took care of the liquor, you and yours by themselves took care of half a case nearly.' "

And in her man's undershirt—Reis, extra large, the elastic scissored under her arms and around her belly so it should not bind or chafe—she rocked and rollicked him till the bed creaked on its casters.

A "Yiden" was heard from his father. Then agonized snoring.

Over which Simon's mother sang in a piercing and buoyant voice,

> *Why are you still mitchin'*
> *Workin' in the kitchen?*
> *Why keep the family waiting?*
> *When we can do the grating?*

"*M' schlagt yiden,*" his father croaked out.

"Bright eyes, little beauty," his mother muttered at him.

To Simon she sang,

> Horlick's Malted Milk
> *Is good for growing children.*

At "children" she wet him with kisses and tears.

Following this they spent a short, sweet time giggling as Simon's father bubbled and burbled, "America" . . . "Greenhorn" . . . "Piecework."

He was doing a *Kaddish* with the force of two cantors when they both together rose, trotted to the window, and stuck out their heads like gargoyles. Over the stupendous clutter of the fire escape—seltzer-bottle valves, day-old rolls wetted down for the birds, a snip of Octagon Soap on an oyster shell, a beach-ball bladder, a *yahrzeit* glass, a curtain rod, a clothespin bag overflowing with pollyseed husks, a lima-bean plant dying in a Diamond Kosher Salt box—they took in the immense heavens over Brighton Beach.

"God's country," his mother chirped.

Immediately Simon was doing, "Bah-bah-bah-*baum-baum-baum*-bah . . . bah . . . bah . . ."

And his mother boosted him on her knee, cried, "Eyes and ears of the world!" and they simultaneously cranked their right arms.

And from their fifth-floor plus stoop, under the good first sun, they panned and picked out Gelfman drawing for himself the first soda of the day; Dopey Duhvee leaning over his tricycle to drool down big, rich spit bombs that burst over his mother's shoes; Mrs. Chepper slipping the leash off her old Pekinese, blaring, "Beauty, don't be in a big hurry, don't force!"; the cripple Fastenberg, who sang on subways, salting his cup with change; the cats of Schactman's Market pawing, delicate as diviners, at the pails of chicken parts; Yenta Gersh, in a cut-down Homburg, blue-satin cocktail dress, and black sneakers dragging her baby buggy up and down and back and forth on the Bay 4 sands, contending with gulls over news-sheets, bottle tops, wooden ice-cream spoons, bathing caps, umbrella handles, kite tails, atomizers, her short-handled one-toothed rake skimming, sifting, sorting, striking like a snake.

"Fill up on it, Shimmy," his mother instructed. "Shimmy Shimmy, take in sweeter and greener memories than your mother has."

Once more she drifted into song.

> It's the pot cheese with a *ta'am*
> It comes right from the farm
> Sweet Maid, Sweet Maid . . .

With tremulous breaths, with a hot and twisted face, she was after a time able to say, "Don't worry, cute tush boy, the ripe time is coming, the whole world is going to get the story of Malvena the Orphan's youthful years . . ."

"Black Hundred," his father announced.

"And all those who shit on her head will hear her finally finally open a mouth."

"Read, Mommy." Simon snapped the waist band of her bloomers. "Mommy read me read me! Journal journal!"

"Even though it's in the drafty stage?"

"Even even though!"

"Remember," his mother begged gently, "that to protect the innocent I made it my business to change certain certain names."

". . . remember."

"Like you could hear the name Darling Soap and it's really . . ."
She winked impishly.

"Sweetheart Soap!"

They had a good laugh on this. Till his father wheezed, "Steerage."

"Dumb old fotz face!" Simon snapped at the bed.

"*Shah, shtill*," his mother chided, dealing out soft blows and love-bites. "Nobody nobody can help how he looks."

To the tune of *We Want Cantor* Simon went

> Read read Read read
> Read read Read read . . .

So on all fours they labored to the foot of the bed. Which Simon's mother raised up and up by a scrolled beast paw while he crawled under and fetched out the *New York Times Illustrated History of the Great War*.

"Okay, outstanding student? Okay A-A-A-Except-in-Gym-Kid?"

"Okay, Mommy."

"Dispensary," his father caroled as his mother, dipping slightly, using only forearm and wrist, softly and soundlessly let down the bed.

"Talk English," his father directed.

"He's a dopey dirty *shmutz*," went Simon.

"Shame shame," his mother honed on her fingers. "On a Daddy you dassn't say 'he.' "

But in a second she and Simon were riffling the brownish folio-size pages, and she was saying, "Zeppelins, zeppelins, again zeppelins, go back to the Kaiser, I'm going back, I see the Kaiser, I see Rasputin, I see the Czar, crosses, crosses, crosses-crosses-crosses, soldiers, soldiers *with* guns and soldiers *without* guns, notice you don't see one Jewish face, now the Czar is already dead, they're having their revolution, let me try again zeppelins, the *goyim* and their zeppelins, he tried yesterday to fool the Mommy, he flushes the toilet she should think he made his big business . . ."

"Brownsville," his father whimpered.

.   .   .

"The Truth of My Life, by Malvena Sloan."

His mother swiftly spread newssheets over the kitchen table, then spread her raft of soft-covered notebooks over the newssheets.

She ceremoniously sniffled, dried both nostrils and one eye with her undershirt.

"What has gone before I don't don't have to tell you."

As though setting himself to hear The Singing Lady Simon shut his eyes slowly and emitted a soft sighing sound.

"When she was left off the Mommy was dealing with her outstanding success achievements in the field of passementerie and telling how with youthful folly, alone in the world at the death of her sweeet sweet mother, she threw away a wonderful little position with Tarshis and Meltzer where she did only only French knots to work for her Cousin Phillie though she knew, and how and how she knew, his *momzer* character and terrible ways covered already in Book Three, Cousin Phillie: *His Momzer Character and Terrible Ways* . . ."

She chewed on a palm; Simon squeezed his eyes into a crimson blindness.

"You're listening, Shimmy? Listen and you won't need any more Stella Dallas."

She raked her cheeks; he bit a knuckle.

"Here—here goes."

She folded back a notebook and jumped to her feet.

" 'Went to Hartford, Connecticut, worked for Cousin Phillie, left same.' "

She plopped down.

"First papers!" his father blared.

"Every every day," his mother cheerily returned, "should be his *yahrzeit.*"

And then she took a stiff shot of breath, saying, "Book Ten. Here is where the Mommy is making many many new friends and keeping company with Victor Mintzer, then business manager for the Yiddish Art Theater but already studying by night toward a future chiropodist profession. She later on comes across him in a chiropodist capacity, where he does a botch job on an ingrown toenail and she goes to Dr. Witkewitz, a big big foot man, to take off your shoe in his office cost those years four dollars. He sends the Mommy on an emergency basis to Dr. Levine, a professor of professors, for a first visit he charged eleven dollars, you asked the doorman, 'Where is Dr. Levine's office?' that was already your first visit. Here we learn how Dr. Levine took one one look at the Mommy's foot and started in about hospitals, X rays, immediate surgery, whirlpool treatments, tests, and how the Mommy cried and kissed his hands and told him, 'Dr. Levine, honey, what are you starting in with hospitals and what are you starting in with whirlpool treatments, realize you're talking to a recent orphan.' Still the Mommy hears from him three hundred for surgery, eight dollars a day special medicine, a needle series twenty-three dollars plus another twenty-three dollars to make sure it's the right needle. And we find out how the Mommy kisses his hands a little more and how she says, 'Professor, dear, my father I never knew, he died in Bolshvetz from complications.' 'Bolshvetz?' 'Bolshvetz.' 'Your father was named Wolf Adler Mendelstern?' 'The same.' 'Go go, *maideleh*, and when you get home put on a little little black salve.' Meanwhile—meanwhile American times are changing and setting the Mommy up for her tragic destiny: There's a big big milk war, they're coming out with vegetable cream cheese, matzo meal is in bags, then it's in boxes, the world is going wild, wild and crazy for the large-curd pot cheese. Here we start seeing, under the section *Cousin Phillie: How He Tried to Hire Me Out to Schvartzers . . .*"

"Lay-off," they heard.

"Tape measure," they also heard.

And the bedroom bloomed with commotion.

"Mommy . . . ?"

"Not yet time."

"G'vald Momma!"

"Heh heh," went Simon, and "Now . . . ?"

"Still not time."

At "BISODOL!" she let Simon enter; while he bounced and jiggled on the bed she was bantering, "Mr. Personality plus" and "Ricardo Cortez number two."

Whereupon his father, a small man with a face of horsey length and a melancholy, popeyed, lopsided look, trembled his hands and feet like a roach trembling its wands and made his rough awakening.

He said, "Ho-boy."

Then, sitting forward in the bed and chuckling with sad merriment, he went on to say, "Rah-bah-boy, listen to a sweet dream. Starts off that I hear—I hear from Kalish and Klein. Shmuel, come back, we'll be open again, we got—ho-boy—a big rush rush order. Nine thousand caps . . ."

"He has six hairs," his mother was telling Simon, "and they all all six have to fall off on the pillow case . . ."

"Nine thousand caps!" cried his father, bitterly moved.

". . . then first he finishes up and he gives a drool on the six hairs."

"Let's say—say they got the order," his father mused. "An order like that and that kind of an order . . ."

A damp pillowcase suddenly engaged his nose.

". . . they could never get the linings," he finished up.

"Next time," Simon's mother said easily, "and you shouldn't live to have a next time, you should float away altogether."

"If I shouldn't live to have a next time," his father answered remotely, "you should live to be a widow."

As she stretched out lazily on the bed Simon's mother replied, "If I should live to be a widow you should first first drop dead."

"If I should drop dead you should get like a floor and once—wuh-hunce a year they should have to come and scrape you."

To which his mother made amiable reply, "If I should get like a floor you should get like an enema bag and they should hang you only only behind doors."

His father, grumbling out some gas, said, "If I should get like an enema bag you should get like an empty store and gypsies should move into you."

"If I should get like an empty store . . ." Simon's mother clapped hands lightly, "*Nu, nu,* Shmuel, you'll be late!"

Right away he rose, threw on a red and black flannelette bathrobe, a *yarmalka* of the same cloth, slung a truss over his shoulder like a bandolier, and padded taut-legged and barefoot to the bathroom.

"Rockaway," he was heard blaring.

He followed this with cries of "Manhattan Beach" and "Niagara Falls" till he worked up his tinkle to a splash.

And twirling the tassel of his bathrobe he emerged, blew a happy kiss at the *mezuzah,* and gave his attention to Simon.

"Barf!" he commanded. "Do for the Daddy a barf and a weep."

"Gong!" went Simon, immediately fisty.

"This," said his father, pulling him till they stood belly to belly, "thi-his is by me a best pal."

"Heh heh," answered Simon.

"He is *my* best pal and I am *his* best pal and both together we'll do—ho-boy!—he-man things. Right?"

"Daddy, wowee Daddy . . ."

"Say better—Pop." He now had Simon by the short neck hairs. "The—Pop."

"Hurts. That that . . ."

"You'll call me the Pop and I'll do like in the Jackie Cooper pictures where the father, the Pop, when he's a best pal by Jackie Cooper he does this, this is what he does, this—thi-his he does to the Jackie Cooper hair, they call it, what they call it . . ."

"Woooo . . ."

"A tousle. A tousle or—a tousling," he rumbled, working with both hands, "and for his tousle a Jackie Cooper boy goes crazy, he even brings home black eyes that the Pop should tousle with him . . ."

"A blood poison!" Simon cried.

"That—ho-boy!—that's when he learns from the Pop how to make with the hands, to barf and weep and throw the jib-jabs. In all the Jackie Cooper pictures you have to have the part where he barfs and weeps and throws the jib-jabs . . ."

He had Simon against the sink, his short arms slamming away, his head butting.

"Shmuel . . ."

Simon's mother flicked a finger at the old nickel of the alarm clock.

His father flung Simon away, saying, "Malvena, I try and I try and still I don't get close to him."

"Dumb dopey moron," his mother answered mildly from the icebox. "What you have to do you don't do. You should make with him what the *goyim* call . . ."

She set before him in single file a lox wing, a whitefish tail, the heel of a farmer cheese, the skin from a sable.

". . . a friendship."

She rolled a Greek olive in a snip of matjes herring and popped it playfully into his mouth.

"You have to go places and you have to do things."

"Why not?" Simon's father answered yearningly. "Rah-boy-oh-boy, let him show me only palship and buddyness and I would meet him half-way, I would be like in the jokes, the fun-loving Pop."

He started a laugh which flew off suddenly into open space.

"What wouldn't I do for him?" he demanded, banging the lox wing against the whitefish tail. "I used to have dreams that on *Yom Kippur* we'd go down to Williamsburg, the Pop and the pal, we'd walk over by the river, we'd have a good cry, and I'd show him how you're supposed to throw your sins in the water . . ."

"The way your Daddy throws sins in the water," his mother told Simon, "nobody can throw sins in the water."

"I have to pay Pinya Friedman a condolence call, I even had in mind"—he doffed his *yarmalka*—"to take him along for the ride. And that's a ride," he added, "wuh-hunce in a lifetime."

"Remember, Gold-Seal-Honor-Card-Kid?" Simon's mother put her hands between Simon's hands. "You were only only four, you wouldn't remember, we took you to the cemetery and you had to had to throw up from the trip." She swayed their hands. "This is even a bigger trip."

She spooned sour cream over half a matzo and pushed it in sections between his father's jaws.

Who made himself heard even over the great strife of his gumming as he said, "I was making plans for regular-guy things that the fun-loving Pop and his American boy pal should be buddy-buddy. One day, maybe, we'd go by Rabbi Leibish, Rabbi Leibish would show him how you take a *trafe* knife and get it kosher again. I'd work in a little side trip. Why not? How many sons I got?" Blinking, squinting, his father momentarily searched the kitchen. "We'd walk over, it's on the way, he could come in with me to the dispensary to renew my clinic card . . ."

"You want him to get a kick out of Leibish?" demanded Simon's mother. "Forget about knives, forget about kosher; you have Leibish do one thing and only only one thing—his pooh-pooh on the evil eye!"

". . . surprise presents. One week—ho-boy!—a Shapiro Wine *Haggadah*, another week a nice white-on-white Sporty Morty type *yarmalka* . . ."

He was out of his chair, dancing around Simon.

"The *Haggadah*," he cried murderously, "he wouldn't look at. To spite me! The *yarmalka*, rah-bah-boy-oh-boy, that's another story. Right? Right, Jackie Cooper face? He'll save it, the Skippy kid, he should have something to wear to the cemetery . . ." With a whole matzo he slashed at Simon. "He should look good when he stands over my grave. Then"—the matzo circled Simon's throat—"he'll have himself, ho-boy, a lovely little ride in the limousine car, a free ride, he'll come home and the first thing . . ."

He feinted for a headlock; Simon, as usual, butted nicely to the crotch.

". . . to read *Toots and Caspar.*"

Simon, weeping cagily, sneaked in a "Schmucky mutt!"

"That's the first thing," said his father with a prideful chuckle, with clubbing motions, "theh-hen, after he eats up all the candy from the basket—three-seventy-nine, it'll come with our society card. Jackie Cooper *momzer*—he'll run see the Tailspin Tommy chapter . . ."

"Were you six? He wasn't even even six," Simon's mother protested softly, "he used to read to the Mommy *Toots and Caspar.*"

And with the heel of her hand she drove Simon's father like a nail into his chair.

To Simon she said, "Who is going to make up with the Daddy and who is going to put him in a happy mood?"

Simon sobbed out *The Pledge of Allegiance.*

"Get killed for Jackie Cooper!" his father told him.

Simon, planting an elbow on the table, made believe he was doing Palmer penmanship, throwing in also the closing hours of the library and the number of books he was allowed on a children's card.

"Get killed with Jackie Cooper."

Simon recited the holiday prices at the Lyric, the day for the changing of bills at the Miramar and the Surf.

"Get killed by Jackie Cooper."

Still he made only the mildest protest when Simon's mother gave them both sour cream from one spoon, and he was already returning her snappy salute as she sprang and capered and chanted

> *Eins, tzvei, drei,*
> You'll be eating *chozerei.*
> They'll shave the beard right off your chin
> So you can chase the Kaiser to Berlin;
> Never mind it you're a Jew-ooh-ooh
> Uncle Sam needs—
> Uncle Sam calls—
> Uncle Sam wants you-ooh-ooh.

His father breasted the table, moving his head one way, his eyes another. A soft, sucking sound escaped his clenched teeth and he said, "Shmuel the Cap Maker. Shmuel the Soldier. Hah-honly yesterday . . ."

"A movie, a movie," went Simon. "*Only Yesterday* is John Boles, it was at the Miramar . . . !"

"In New York I was a nothing. But in the army"—his father tried to snap his fingers—"all of a sudden, like the . . . scholar big shot of the company."

". . . they had it with *Guns of the Pecos* at the Miramar. But when it came down from the Miramar you know what they had it with? Heh? Heh!" piped Simon.

"I had to be the ha-whole Jewish history expert. How come the Jews started the war, how the Jews got all the money in the world, what kind of blood we use when we make matzo . . ."

"*The World Moves On*," Simon announced. "That was Paul Muni, that was Aline McMahon . . ."

"Where I got the biggest kick . . ."

His father charged off the chair.

"To hear how they talk. It's worth teh-hen armies to hear how they talk."

He had his *yarmalka* over his brows, his head bowed, his arms dangling.

"Shee-yut!" he cried.

And as Simon and his mother whinnied and swelled with mirth he gave them a "Fah-hark you!"

"I have to hold myself back," said his mother, panting and turning away. "Otherwise it gets me right in my dropped stomach."

Laughing also, his father burbled. "Has to come back . . . if I can remember."

"With your ear," declared Simon's mother, "I'm not not worried."

"In my company alone I must have had—I had—ho-boy!—three, four kinds *goyim*."

Hugging herself, then hugging his father, Simon's mother said, "Shmuel, Shmuel, ten good days I probably never had from you, two weeks definitely not. From the minute I met you you had heartburn. When you don't get a diarrhea you're plugged up solid. For an intermission—nosebleeds. You never had nothing to give and if you had something you wouldn't give it anyway. In every every way you come out a failure, a lacking, personality, a strict nix, and in general I would be better off if before I met you I went down with the *Titanic* together. But one thing you have and one thing you got . . ."

She pinched his belly.

". . . a natural natural ear."

"We're hearing first and first we'll hear . . ."

Bending under the sink, Simon's father flipped open the bread box.

". . . a soldier from the South."

He came up with a clothespin on his nose.

"What the *goyim* call—a Southerner."

"It isn't only a natural ear," his mother was explaining to Simon, "it's his knack."

"Knack is a *K*-word," Simon winningly whined. "You know, Mommy?"

And his father twanged, "Dixie, farton-rarton-darton-on-a-carton, Dixie!"

"Picture if that had training," his mother brooded.

"Theh-hen he meets a buddy from the West—the . . . West. They go, the buddies, to what the *goyim* call . . ." his father stamped a foot at Simon. "One word, Jackie Cooper killer. One word—a little word—a *goyish* word."

"By *goyim* the most important word," his mother cued.

"In the cowboy pictures they have it," said Simon, smiling away. "A"—he waited for his mother's kiss—"bar."

"They go-ho into their—BAR and the Western buddy goes, how he goes is . . ."

Simon's father tore away the clothespin.

"Range, beer-and-cantaloupe, range!"

Then he bobbed his head, accepting the applause and two spoonfuls more of sour cream.

And after a spell of silence he had this to say:

"From the army I found out a thing about the *goyim* and that thing I carry on me all my life. *Goyim* are veh-hery handy."

"That's why you have to have them," asserted Simon's mother.

"I don't say the *schvartzers* aren't handy. If they want to be— naturally they don't always want to be—they can be handier than the *goyim*."

"When you have a jar and the jar is stuck your best bet is a *schvartzer,*" said Simon's mother. "They know, they have it in them, and their one little twist is the right twist."

"Ho-boy, when it comes to jars—forget it! Forget it, because you can't do better than a *schvartzer,*" his father conceded. "But if you need him where he has to be handy on the animals . . ."

He filled the kitchen with a Bronx cheer.

"You go to the movies, you see already how the goyim are with horses. They're good with horses—ho-boy are they good!—but they're better with cows."

"They're by the cows," his mother explained to Simon, "the way *schvartzers* are by the jars."

"But—buh-hut, when it comes to chickens I'll take a Jew any time. *Any* time. A Jew goes over by a chicken, the chicken likes him—fine. The chicken doesn't like him? That's too bad because a Jew wants to be liked by a chicken. He would rather be liked, but if he's not liked—also fine. He don't lose sleep over it, he don't—cater. With the *goyim,* they go near a chicken and right away they start catering."

"Remember, Teacher's-Blackboard-Cleaner-Kid, you had it once in a song"—his mother made Simon clap hands—"a *goy,* a farm, a *goyisher* farmer, how he catered to the chickens, chick-chick *du,* chick-chick *dort, du* a chick, *dort* a chick . . ."

"You see a Jew doing that?" demanded his father. "*Balt!* He'll take care of a chicken, he'll feed a chicken—believe me, he'll feed it better then the *goy*—but he won't take shit from a chicken. And the *goyim* realize it, don't think they don't. They're dumb, but they're not blind."

Bitter, rueful, Simon's mother said, "Maybe if we handled chickens with more *finekeit* they wouldn't have it in for us the way they have it in for us."

"Ho-boy, don't kid yourself," his father answered judiciously. "With them to us it's a case of—you know what?—jealousy. They're jealous of us with our chickens the way we're jealous of them with their cows. And we got—believe me we got what to be jealous. Because you go out of New York, you first see what rich milk is."

To herself, Simon's mother said, "Malvena Malvena, you'd be be better off if it wasn't so rich."

To Simon, she said, "It's in my Book Four, Part Two: *Cousin Phillie and How He Gets Malvena the Orphan to Go to Hartford, Connecticut, by Telling Her That When She Gets Out of New York*

She'll First See What Rich Milk Is."

While she wept Simon pulled at her undershirt and cupped her ear, and they passionately whispered together.

". . . with real real expression," he said aloud, kissing both pinkies.

"Remember," he was warned, "this is a holy holy swear and you're swearing on the Mommy's dropped stomach."

"*Yisgadol, vyiskadash*, boobooboo, how I'll do it . . ."

Whereupon his mother pushed Simon against his father, saying, "Shmuel, listen to something cute. The Good-Note-From-His-Teacher-Kid has a bargain that if you do for him your special specialty he'll do over you a *Kaddish* with his wonderful expression . . ."

". . . have to be up to it first," Simon protested. "We don't do it in Hebrew till way way later."

"I heard *Kaddish*," cried his father. "*Shiva* I didn't hear."

His mother, nodding and nodding with all her might, said simultaneously to Simon, "*Shiva* is where you don't have to do a thing, *Shiva* is where you just just sit and take it easy."

"Blech," went Simon, and "Yuch."

"For seven days!" his father howled. "You could say, like—a week!"

"And for those seven days you dassn't dassn't read the jokes," his mother reminded. But as Simon put his underlip forward and puffed out his cheeks she added hastily, "He can never never take a tease, he doesn't know the Mommy is doing a tease, doesn't he know the Mommy would put the jokes away for him, the Mommy wouldn't touch them and the Mommy would save them . . ."

"It's what the *goyim* call—a mourning," his father pointed out heartily.

"That that's an antonym word," Simon yelled at his mother, "that's A, N, T, O . . ."

"WODDER!"

His father, suddenly in character, clumped around the kitchen, tamped down an imaginary pipe at the side of his mouth.

"Cohen flakes," he cried.

"I notice something now," his mother told Simon. "It's not just his ear."

"Carfee!"

"It's his ear and it's more than his ear," his mother reasoned.

"The *goyim* are in their TOWN, they decide they are GOIN to town, you'll drop dead before you hear a G from a *goy* . . ."

"He lives on *Ex-Lax* and *Feenamint*, but give him give him only rich foods. From the day he was born he looked like he needed a rest. If he was a building he would have been by now condemned. But he has what Moishe Lufthandler had when Moishe Lufthandler was in his prime: The timing!"

"One—wuh-hun *goy* walks down by his Main Street and he meets the other *goy*, the both *goyim* are going to their"—his father winked and twitched at Simon—"from before. The one word—the little word . . ."

"Bar," went Simon.

" 'Heh-lo there . . . Jim.' 'Heh-lo there . . . Roy.' "

"Just just to remember those names," murmured Simon's mother.

" 'Tell me . . . Jim . . . Jim, what is doing and what is new by your wife MARY?' 'My wife, MARY, is much better, she is straightening up in the . . . church. But how is your bi-hig dog Killer?' 'My big dog Killer is fine, and what do you think whether it will . . . rain?' 'Well, it mi-hight rain, also it mi-hight *not* rain.' 'Let's hope and let's pray it should only rain for the rain is good on . . . the grass.' "

He started tittering, soon broke up completely.

"Give them—ho-boy!—give them a bar and give them—THE GRASS!"

"You'll go out of New York," his mother said to Simon, "you'll see them with their grass."

"Grass—grassgrassgrass," barked his father. And in great good humor he fed Simon farmer cheese and sable skin from off his fingers, calling him "Kiddo" and "Little Doughboy" and snapping out tricky questions.

He said, "My manager did it on me, I'll do it on you. Let me—leh-het's hear which one weighs more—the pound of feathers or the pound of coal."

"Feathers—coal. That's a *pound* of feathers and a *pound* of coal, the *feathers* are a pound and the *coal* is a pound . . ."

". . . have to use common sense."

"A pound, each one is a pound, the feathers *and* the coal . . ."

"H-only the common sense."

". . . the samesameexactthing!" Simon cried gloriously.

"For that he has to come close and he has to stand right by the Pop," his father said softly, "and he has to get his Jackie Cooper tousle."

"Heh heh," Simon went.

"Rah-bah-boy-oh-boy," replied his father, stepping back and sighting along his hand, "this is a tall kid, he's going with the Pop soon in the tall-kid department, ho-boy this is going to be what you got to call a TALL KID."

And he right away started springing and slapping, slapping and pinching, with pain in his voice saying, "*Oy*, he'll be taller than me . . ."

In two seconds Simon's mother had him in hand, shaking him like a can of scouring powder over the sink.

"Latey-latey, Shmuel," she gaily sang.

At once his father popped up from the chair and clomped to the bedroom, on his way undressing; he was, before shutting the door in their faces, down to *yarmalka* and truss.

"What the Daddy had to go through . . ."

"Crazy cockee nut," went Simon.

". . . you should never never have to know from Second-Highest-In-Achievement-Test-Kid."

His father rapped on the bedroom door, crying, "He should so!"

"When this was with Kalish and Klein this was altogether a different person. This had a one-in-a-million cap face. This used to model for buyers . . ."

"With the flah-haps *on* the face and the flaps *away* from the face," came from his father.

"Then first at his age to start learning the usher trade, don't don't think it's so easy, you have to know where the loge is and you have to know where the orchestra is . . ."

"And what about the searchlights?" his father trumpeted tearily. "Go figure they need two—two batteries."

"Even if now and then once in a while he gets a little little"— Simon's mother warped her face, waggled her tongue, and smacked herself alongside her head—"nervous, you should never forget that this is a forgotten vet."

"Let him sometimes ask me"—His father stuck his face out the door—"What—wah-haht price glory?"

"The Mommy is a little little mixed up about what happened, when he got taken by the army," his mother began, "and I can't tell you exactly if two days before his sister got knocked down by a Sparkling Seltzer truck or a Vitality Seltzer truck."

Amid spells of weeping his mother made them matzo and sour-cream sandwiches and gave him to understand "how the army had fixed and *futzed* his father. How *erev Slichus*, on his grand-mother's *yahrzeit*, fourteen-and-a-half years after his parents had been moved by the Wishneff Van Corporation (three broken-down pushcarts, two healthy Polacks) from 199 Eldridge Street to 40B Eldridge Street, three blocks from what was then the Langman Surgical Supply Store, now the Langman Surgical Supply Outlet, right across the street from the stoop where Moey Amsterdam, secretary-treasurer of the Knickers Makers Union, Local 18, would soon have his face scarred by gangster acid, he having been mis-taken for Sam Pomerantz, a nothing in the Markers and Pullers Joint Board, the army had sent his father to either North Carolina or South Carolina. How he had been assigned there to egg candling. How on the second day of *Tisha B'Av* disturbed by a piece of bad news from home (Lilyveld, the Painter, had chipped his mother's cut-glass bowl), and further unsettled by sight of a blood spot in one brown jumbo, he had suffered a fit, a conniption, a prostration, an itchiness in the scalp. How doctors by the bunch had given him million-dollar examinations. How they had brought down one specialist for a tsuttzing. ('What what do you say, Doctor?' 'Tsutt, tsuttz, tsuttz . . .') How he had fallen finally into the best of hands. (A Jewish doctor.) How this top-notch surgeon had come in smil-ing after the second exploratory. ('We'll take a few few more X rays to be absolutely positive, but the way I see it, my friend, it's definitely a *dybbuk*.') How he had been sent back to his eggs. How on November 11, 1918, the twenty-second anniversary of his Uncle Chaim Yitschak's departure from Pilkaboldrovnyiecz to Strobleki by way of Nova-Hanakye, a road close to Biriprog, where her own mother had been born, his nerves shot to pieces by his sister's last postcard (Lilyveld had stinted on a second coat of pot-cheese white in the closets), he had sent down the candling chute a few too many eggs. How they had burst around him and upon him. How this had shocked his system. How the army, in consequence, had been forced to declare him . . ."

". . . a shell-shock case."

And his mother squatted down before the bread box like a Chinaman, telling Simon in a tear-crippled voice, "I'll show you, Advanced-Reading-And-Spelling-Kid, how he got a beautiful beau-tiful write-up in the *Yeshivah Ram Bam News*, look look at the bag

Teitlebaum gives you for nine cans of King Oscar sardines, can he spare it, I'm going down later and I'll throw it in his face, remind me to ask him for an extra key . . ."

There was a stern knocking, then a "Don't—do-hon't look everybody!"

Head lowered, eyes raised, blaring "Puh-lenty standing room only!" Simon's father shambled over and presented arms with a fat flashlight. He had on a black shako, a washed-out looking serge tunic with blue and gold piping and button-down pockets, white duck shorts and white Keds cut open at the toes; a pair of pink elastic bandages braced him in the ankles.

"I have to have one kiss from it," cried Simon's mother, swooping in, getting one kiss and giving back five.

His father, all excited and shining the flashlight, announced, "Now playing the fir-hirst time second run"—he peeped into a pocket—"*Storm over the Bengal.*"

"Mommy, you know what a Bengal is? Heh, Mommy?" went Simon. "Bomba Katz told it, a joke . . ."

"Short wait for immediate seating."

"A Bengal is a LITTLE BANG!"

"Take—tah-hake only one program."

Opening her arms, his mother scooped in Simon and his father, whispering, "It's my my little family unit and nobody else's."

She was answered by a "Heh heh" and a "Ho-boy!"

Then she made Simon link and lock fingers with his father, and she led them in a little dance on the blue squares and on the white squares of the linoleum, saying, "You'll tell me Malvena Malvena keep quiet and bite your tongue, but I feel on my dropped stomach that for this family unit good times are just just around the corner."

She was answered by a "Heh heh" and a "Rah-bah-boy, I'm willing to walk a block."

And she made them dance to her right and dance to her left while she said further, "Where I look I see the Depression is getting to be a lost cause. You'll say to me, 'Malvena Malvena, you're such an optimist, how come the marshals moved out Mrs. Shefsel with all her furniture?' and I'll tell you, 'How come her couch had brand-new slip covers?' "

She was answered by a "Heh heh" and a "That's—tha-hat's why Daddy Warbucks lost millions!"

And she moved them clockwise, then counterclockwise, saying, "Then first I get a dream about my sweet sweet Momma, she's calling me from the street, she has a message for me from Uncle Chaim Getzel in heaven that it's good-bye and good luck Mister Hard Times and that I should spend on myself a little, I should get wax paper in the big rolls. And while I'm running to the window she starts in singing, 'Potatoes are cheaper, tomatoes are cheaper . . .' "

She was answered by a "Heh heh" and a "I wouldn't mind already vegetables and sour cream."

And she had them swing their arms in and swing their arms out, saying, "I begged her, 'Sweet sweet Momma darling, could you give me a prosperity sign?' And right right there I saw on the fire escape two beautiful little jars, you couldn't get them two for a nickel, and in each jar there were Octagon coupons."

She got back a "Fartzy Daddy Fotz!" and a "Choke on a charlotte russe, Jackie Cooper killer!"

Crying copiously and warning about her dropped stomach, she waded in and very soon had Simon's father gentled.

"You'll walk with him, Shmuel, you'll love it and you'll enjoy it, the kid walks with the Daddy to work, you'll build up our little family unit and you'll make the whole whole world jealous."

To Simon, his mother said, "Who has a Mommy that when he comes back from his Daddy and kid walk is going to give him a beautiful beautiful rubberband for his rubberband gun?"

"Ho-sure," his father grumped. "I walk with the Jackie Cooper face, I meet my cap-trade buddies, that's all I need."

"What he does when he walks—you know what he does, Mommy?" Simon's eyes were hooded. "He—like this—he bunks me . . ."

"They see him," his father said triumphantly, "I'm out—I'm finished in the union. And I wouldn't blame them. Because the day Jackie Cooper went in with a naked head to get a hair tousle—that day murdered off the cap trade."

His mother had each of them by an arm, lamenting as she moved them to the door, "Bear in mind how I'm not a well woman . . ."

"Even in *Skippy*," his father mused, "in *Skippy* where he wears himself a cap he makes sure—only a brimless."

". . . I don't tell you everything, how I had to call Mrs. Harlib into Teitlebaum yesterday, she should please please squeeze the rolls for me."

His mother's groans kept them company all the way to the second floor. Where Simon's father beat against Mrs. Shura's peep hole and sought to know if it had been her Lillian who last week popped bubble gum three times in his general direction.

On the ground floor he stopped Mrs. Landes to give her a first fair warning about steaming up the super against him.

By the Brighton Beach El he paused while a train lumbered and slammed into the station, then gave strict instructions that the motorman should take it easy, that he had Jewish lives in his hands.

In silence he passed Magid's Shoe Outlet, Nagelsteen's Imperial Yarn, Madame Schnall's Electrolysis Parlor, and the Apron Emporium. By the window of Schneider's Royal Yarn he braked, then in speedy slow motion doffed his shako, opened two buttons on his tunic, beat upon Simon's head with both fists, hung all his weight on Simon's neck, and sneezed a light sneeze.

Waiting as long as he could, Simon said, "*Leyben.*"

His father built up another sneeze.

"*Leyben*, pull an ear," said Simon.

His father, following a short rest, managed to sniffle.

". . . both ears."

"Ho-boy!"—his father cracked him in the face—"I'm getting a cold."

While Simon wailed softly his father begged him to finish off the job now or in the next few days, before the burial society mailed postcards for the next quarter's dues. "Killer," he said kindly, "murder type. Save yourself a little expense, keep more for Jackie Cooper pictures. You'll live nice, you'll have it—ho-boy!—you'll have it good. You'll go out, you'll buy the *Sunday News*, you'll get *goyish* cup cakes by Dugan's . . ."

"Waha! I'll get? Who'll get?"

"*Who'll get*," his father mimicked. "Jackie Cooper will get."

He hustled Simon along, notifying him that he had been all this time keeping a little blue notebook with red lines, and in this notebook he was putting down with an Eagle pencil Simon's fresh-mouth snot-nose record, that this record would stay a black and blue mark against Simon's life which, with *Raboynoy-shel-oylom's* help, would be anyway a short one.

In this fashion and without further incident they covered the more than half-a-block to the Lyric. Yahrblum the Manager, a large-lipped caracul-headed man with rolls of healthy fat under his sleeveless golfer's sweater, was already bouncing his barker's cane on the sidewalk and shouting sonorously at the El, "Four stars in the *Daily News*, four, so help me, Kate Cameron says, 'A superb history drama,' Mandel of the *Forvitz* writes 'You'll enjoy,' the Magid of Vilna puts it this way, 'Harm it can't do,' a dime until five, better than doctors, hello there Shmuel Sloan and son, *Badland Bullets* is the second feature, somewhere else it would be a main feature, very glad you could make it, Shmuel, ten cents, the Coming Attractions alone should cost more, how is my best-looking head usher?"

He winked at Simon, then said, "Hey, Shmuel, you're still such a hoo-ha hotsy-totsy Roosevelt man?"

Simon's father drew himself up to a slouch.

"I'll explain why I ask . . ."

Yahrblum gave Simon a powerful goose.

"I ask because I heard today some shocking, shocking news. I was told by this party, his name is out—in fact, I shouldn't tell you, but if a manager dassn't tell his best-looking head usher it's no America—I was told reliably that . . ."

His smile spread wider.

"I heard . . ."

He cuffed at Simon's crotch.

"Shmuel, I'll ask again, not as your manager, as a friend. A good friend who doesn't want to see you hurt. Did you think it over, did you reconsider, or are you still *ay-ay-ay* for Roosevelt?"

"For Roosevelt—for Roosevelt pluh-hus his missus," Simon's father cried hotly.

"Then your manager is the bearer of bad news. Because I was informed"—Yahrblum drew Simon and his father behind the ticket booth—"the reliable source told me"—he swished his cane operatically—"Roosevelt . . . that Mr. Roosevelt . . . sucks."

"Roosevelt sucks?"

"Believe it, Shmuel."

"Couldn't be a mistake. Couldn't be—ho-boy!—you heard he sucks, you didn't hear on what he sucks?"

"He doesn't believe his manager," Yahrblum told Simon bitterly, gently. Then, "Your manager tells you, Shmuel, believe your manager. Roosevelt . . . sucks!"

"Roosevelt sucks?"

"Roosevelt sucks!"

"I feel"—in sorrowful acknowledgement Simon's father shook his head—"for the missus."

"And the kids?"

Simon's father went into hiccups.

"Your manager himself didn't want to believe. Your manager had to first get the"—Yahrblum flashed a small white card—"documentary evidence."

Using his flashlight, Simon's father read. "*The Yellow Stream*, by I. P. Daley.*"

"Turn over, Shmuel."

"Even so, this is labor's beh-hest friend."

"Your manager gave you an order, Shmuel. Shmuel, turn over!"

"I'm turning, I'm reading, ho-boy, I see already—in green print!"

Then his father showed his teeth to Simon, saying, "Don't tell the Mommy, we don't need to hurt her."

"Nah."

"You're a *momzer* murderer, you hated his guts from the beginning, but even you didn't wish it!"

"Nah, nah Daddy."

He pushed Simon off the curb, saying, "Go, ho-boy, go, Tom Mix and his Tony are calling you!"

And as Simon started to cross his father came after, crying, "Killer-type, you walk away, you don't kiss a Daddy bye-bye?"

Though they held up traffic, though Kushey Kravitz and his older brother, Pinnie, had just then come by and stood looking and laughing, Simon kissed and was kissed. And lingered till his father limped off into the *Lyric* behind Yahrblum.

from

Annihilation

Piotr Szewc

We are on Listopadowa, the second street crossing Lwowska. In one of the tiny backyards close to the intersection, Mr. Hershe Baum is standing near the house and feeding pigeons perched on his arm. Here they are called Persian butterflies. Isn't it a beautiful name? In all likelihood they were brought from Persia. But is that certain? We won't be able to verify it. Data, documents, and credible explanations are unavailable. Supposedly the pigeons can fly for many hours at a height that makes them invisible to the human eye. But since we received this information from a merely casual acquaintance, we cannot vouch for its accuracy. We haven't been interested in such matters. It is beyond doubt, however, that Mr. Hershe Baum's pigeons are highly valued by local pigeon breeders. One often sees buyers of his birds. Now, at the peak of the season, the pigeons draw high prices.

A horse-drawn wagon loaded with sacks passes by. It's only logical to assume it carries grain—a flour mill is located on Listopadowa, and the cart is going in that direction. As our eyes follow the cart, the sun, reflected off a window that someone is opening, blinds us. Soon, through the half-opened window, an extended hand pours the contents of a chamber pot. The whole scene takes only a few seconds. Before we can notice it, the pigeons, scared by the clatter of the wagon, fly off Mr. Hershe Baum's arm. And the hens cackle loudly when the contents of Kazimiera M's pot lands on them. It was Kazimiera M who poured what was in the pot out the window. Although it's warm, Kazimiera M carefully closes the window. For a moment we see her white gown through the windowpane.

Most likely she went to sleep late, and now, after she has emptied the pot, she will want to lie down for at least half-an-hour or so. Sleep is best the morning after a busy night. To keep the sun out, Kazimiera M decides to draw the curtains. Even if we wanted, we couldn't peek into her apartment. So let's allow Kazimiera M a well-deserved rest.

Mr. Hershe Baum, who until this minute was standing near the house, shoos away the pigeons clamoring for more grain and ambles into the street. He picks up an apple, one of many scattered in front of the house, and standing outside the opened gate, he brings the apple to his mouth. It has a nice tart taste. With his free hand, he shades his eyes. He contemplates the sun, which has already reached the trees behind the brewery. For the last few days the sun has been unusually bright.

Mr. Hershe Baum calls his wife out of the apartment. Now, shading their eyes, both look at the sun. It takes only a moment. Then Mrs. Baum drops her hand and returns to the apartment. Her husband closes the gate and follows. From here we can see a narrow ribbon of brown smoke escape from the chimney pipe. Unstirred by the slightest breeze, it rises weightlessly, straight up. And since we are still on Listopadowa, we see small panicles of burned paper glide through the air, settle on leaves and grass, then rise again and soar above the trees. Soon the chimney pipe of the Baums' cast-iron stove starts spewing out lighter colored clouds of smoke, which the pigeons, agitated by Mr. Baum, immediately scatter. If it weren't for the unquestionable presence of a mild smell of burning, as well as the soot and ashes that cover the leaves, nobody would suspect that a few minutes ago smoke was emerging from the chimney.

Those few minor events most likely will not influence future events universally considered most significant. The minor events will vanish in the turmoil surrounding more important events and will not be salvaged by memory or photographs. They belong to the past that isn't studied—they are question marks left by each successive generation. Like burned paper, they, together with similar facts and circumstances, will turn to dust scattered in time.

In a week or two or a month Mr. Hershe Baum, the owner of the fabric store that we'll soon have a chance to see, will not even remember last night's nightmarish dream, which he didn't expect or deserve. In his dream the town was flooded. Human heads floated in the water—his own, his wife Zelda's, and their five children's—surely the heads of half the people in town. Strangely enough the water was clear, bloodless, and instead of grass, algae were visible under the surface.

For the foreseeable future we shouldn't ignore all those minor events that are occurring before our eyes. They not only form a unique background for those most important events but presumably they also influence them and will influence them in some way. Mr. Baum's dream, for example, is an extremely bad omen for him.

In the meantime Kazimiera M appears again. She has drawn the curtains apart. Dreamily she opens the window, then raises her hands and stretches. For a moment she freezes, yet right away we see the rhythmic movement of her breasts beneath the nightgown. She twists her long brown hair around her fingers, lifts it above her head, and lets it slowly fall onto her shoulders and back.

At the same time, Mr. Hershe Baum, the mercer, walks into Lwowska and heads for the market square. He must be hurrying to his store to open it on time. Kazimiera M, still standing within our vision, combs her hair at the window, while Attorney Walenty Danilowski slowly closes the swinging door to Rosenzweig's tavern.

We are at the edge of the market square, where Lwowska begins. One of us takes a picture. The photographer can shoot at will. Only the width of the lens curbs his freedom. The world is frozen for a fraction of a second. What do we see after the film is developed? Unnatural, somewhat grotesque figures of passersby and of a bicyclist. Two policemen are entering the tavern. The swinging door hasn't quite closed. Through the crack we see a raised hand holding a beer stein.

Many years later someone will leaf through an old photo album. But something will be amiss: the photographs didn't record details, seemingly insignificant, yet important and interesting for the person who looks at the pictures. What we can see now from close up will be invisible or unidentifiable in the photo: the photo doesn't reveal the grimace of confusion or surprise on the face of the bicyclist.

Unfortunately, the photo omits other details as well.

It is impossible to say whether it is Attorney Danilowski who is holding the beer stein in Rosenzweig's tavern. Future close-up techniques would prove that the hand indeed belongs to this gentleman. The cut and the color of the cuff (dark green check) and the number (two) of the buttons would testify to that.

Something else is in the picture.

In the left-hand corner a shapeless spot is visible. Standing in the market square, we know that it is a little black-haired girl. Since we are witnessing the events captured by the photo, we see more than people who will be leafing through the photo album over half-a-century later.

They will detach the pictures and examine them closely. And what will they see? Here someone raises a beer stein or a glass; here someone bikes; here a woman stands, her back turned, her head bent to the side. In the upper left-hand corner a grey spot shows—what could it be? Perhaps clothes hung out to dry? Perhaps a child? They don't know. Frustrated, they stick the photo back in the slits on the page and close the album. For a while longer the images remain in their minds, but we can be sure that those images will soon be forgotten.

The policemen whom we saw entering Rosenzweig's tavern are now comfortably sprawled out on the benches alongside a large table. They comment on last night's events—in fact there weren't any events worth their while—and now and then they wet their lips with beer foam. The sight of the policemen drinking beer should surprise no one: it's early morning and they have the right to feel tired after night duty. As a matter of fact, they aren't here by themselves, although the tavern is still almost empty. They glance at Attorney Danilowski, sitting nearby, and time after time wink wryly at each other. But Mr. Walenty Danilowski seems not to notice and orders another beer. When he visits the tavern, during its least crowded hours, he tries to forget his ailing liver, which to his dismay often demands a special diet. According to his doctor's advice, the attorney should abstain from alcohol. But he enjoys the beer served by the owner of the tavern, beer which is justly famous for going straight to the head.

Both policemen are young and, as usual, ready to crack coarse jokes. That isn't surprising: during the hours of their night duty, they have an opportunity to observe many things never seen by most residents. Attorney Danilowski decides not to pay attention to the policemen, to ignore their presence as far as possible. "Did Kazimiera remember to give the attorney something stronger? A glass of slivovitz to cheer up." After saying this, one of the policemen, Antoni Wrzosek, lifts his beer stein towards Mr. Danilowski as if to drink a toast. In response the attorney emphatically clears his throat and takes a noisy sip of his beer. Let them make such remarks somewhere else in town—in the street maybe but not here, for God's sake, not here!

Offended by this apparent lack of tact, Attorney Danilowski leaves the unfinished beer and, vigorously pushing the door, exits the tavern. Maybe he's returning home. Or maybe he's going to his office since it's his habit to start work early.

For the policemen, for Mr. Hershe Baum, for Kazimiera M, for Attorney Danilowski, and for those now present at the market square—as well as for all the other residents—their town in its microcosmic scale is the model of the universe: with the arm of the river encircling it to the south, with its mesh of streets, its shrines, and its orchards. The Town Hall, the church, and the market square form the center where the ritual of life is enacted. We can assume that all those people are wholeheartedly convinced that they live in the *true* center. Other towns, rivers, and unknown people, separated from them by time and space, are like ripples made by a pebble that someone has thrown in the water.

As early as five in the morning, the sharp rays of the July sun turn the market square into an arena for a spectacular display of chiaroscuro. Filtered through leafy branches, the rays cast vibrant and unreal images onto the pavement. Where the images vibrate, the shadows of houses, stores, and market stalls blend into dark rectangles crowned with roof points. Similar images can be seen on the walls and windows of houses, stalls, and stores overgrown with vines. And such images can be seen now, although the clock struck five a long time ago. (*A long time ago for whom? How long?*)

In the door to one of the stores we see Mr. Hershe Baum. A sign saying FABRIC STORE hangs above the door and the window. The market square isn't busy yet. Occasionally Mr. Hershe Baum gestures or says something to invite passersby to visit the store. What a selection of fabrics! Mr. Baum is extremely pleased with the last shipment he received from Lvov. The open shutters display a sampling of fabrics.

The southern wall of Mr. Baum's store—like the walls of other buildings and stores—is overgrown with vines. They stretch across the roof and fall over the windows on the opposite side. We can hear sparrows chirping and hopping among the creepers.

Mr. Baum enters the store and disappears into its dark interior. For a moment, through the window, we see his head before the shelves of fabric.

We are accompanied by the ubiquitous smell of rotting wood and dank boards, a smell which is trapped in the market square.

Just now, Attorney Danilowski is passing Saint Augustine's Church. He takes a watch out of his pocket. It's three minutes to seven.

Attorney Danilowski isn't in a hurry; he has a lot of time. It won't take more than twenty minutes to get to his office. According to the blue sign posted on the door, the office isn't supposed to open until eight. In a little store opposite the church the attorney buys mints. He puts one into his mouth and stuffs the rest, wrapped in paper, into his pocket. He's expecting a visit from a certain tenant who lives near Zwierzyniec.

The tenant announced his impending arrival by letter. The attorney has already reviewed the case once—it's quite common and rather uninteresting. Today, his client writes, he will hear new details which will supposedly throw more light—but will they really?—on the progress of the case.

Unfortunately, this is not the greatest way to spend the morning. The attorney would like to return to Rosenzweig's tavern for another beer, or stop by at Kazimiera M's, even though the time isn't convenient. The latter option is more enticing, but he doesn't turn back. He merely puts another mint into his mouth.

It looks like the day will be hot—probably as hot as the past few days. Dew still covers the grass. The morning is beautiful. The dome of the church glistens copper gold. The parish priest closes the door of the sacristy and walks toward the presbytery. A droshky passes the church. The cabman whips the horses and the droshky disappears into the nearest cross street. A dog that was barking stops for a while but soon starts again, louder this time and closer.

The two policemen leave Rosenzweig's tavern. The younger of them wipes beer foam off his mustache. The policemen's shoes shine in the morning sun although at night they should have gathered at least a thin layer of dust. Their heels rhythmically kick the pavement. In the general din their steps sound like the measured ticking of a clock.

The policeman who has just wiped his mustache asks one of the passersby to tell him the time. "It's almost seven, Sir," the passerby says and raises his hat. The policemen agree that they should report to the police station by eight.

Right now we can see them approaching the market stalls. This is the time of day when business is most brisk. We can hear cackling chickens and the raised voices of vendors. Farther, in the back of the place where poultry is sold, in a small patch between the furrier's stall and the tailor's, clay pots are displayed for sale.

Some have a brown shiny glaze, but most have their natural color. The policemen pass the vendors of poultry and of clay pots. A Gypsy woman, who had been telling two women their fortunes, is now dragging a little boy who clutches her skirt. Suddenly she disappears from our view. The policemen don't see her either. They look at and taste the fruit that they take out of the vendors' baskets. For a moment they hesitate. Then they buy a bag of sour cherries.

Hungry pigeons sneak among the laid-out goods. They peck at scattered lentils and linseed. They are audacious and dauntless.

The attorney sighs deeply. For a moment he feels a freezing chill on his lips as if the needles of mentholated hoarfrost settled on his tongue, lips, and palate. Mentholated hoarfrost, so much like the one many years ago, back in—it's incredible—but why count the years? Attorney Danilowski thinks again about Rosenzweig's tavern when he was twelve, or thirteen, or maybe fourteen years old. In the mouth of the boy who has been sucking mints the green mentholated needles turn into green interwoven with white as if in a watercolor. It was freezing cold when they were on their way to town. They could hear trees cracking. The frail cherry trees behind Rosenzweig's tavern were covered with frost, white, glassy, and crunchy if pressed. A strong eastern wind was blowing; it was Christmas Eve for the Eastern Orthodox, and the faithful were going to church. The two black horses shifted their weight, poked their noses in the snow, stomped, neighed, snorted out drops of spittle that instantly froze into crystals. On their nostrils, necks, and backs, white foam froze—Grandfather forgot to cover the horses with a blanket. Walek didn't go to the tavern, but with other boys romped around it. Yelling, they slid on the ground and threw snow at one another. Walek gave them mints that his grandfather had bought at the tavern. He had bought Walek a bag of anise drops as well but gave them to him on the way home. The boys chewed the mints or sucked them greedily and quickly so that they would get more, as if they were tasting such candy for the first time. Soon mentholated needles appeared around the mouth and on the fuzz which had already sprouted above the upper lip. They licked them and wiped them with their sleeves—the mentholated needles, light green interwoven with white, like frost on the boughs of the cherry trees, like leaves painted by frost on the windowpane and scraped off with a fingernail.

A white, thick, impenetrable layer of frost covered the tavern windows and the windows of the houses that stood behind the tavern on both sides of Gminna Street. Walek and the boys tried to peek inside, blowing on the windowpane or scratching the tangled-up, icy web. Then they blew on their reddened hands—which, it seemed, were about to freeze to the windowpane—put them under their sheepskin coats, and if that didn't help, into their mouths.

The snow lay high, reaching the knees, unbeaten except for a net of paths left by the pedestrians' shoes. It was hard and sharp; an icy crust had formed on its surface, which crunched at every step. The boys avoided the paths, looking for the places where they could plunge into the snow up to the waist, grab huge icy chunks, and throw them at one another, not aiming, blindly counting on luck. The dry and rustling snow sprinkled their coats and dropped inside their shirts where it melted and flowed down their warmed-up backs. Even the gloves and the boots were wet inside.

The horses, freed from the shaft, dipped their heads into the hay which the grandfather had loaded into the sleigh. Their bells jingled and sounded like the snow when the boys' feet crushed it. The boys' voices floated like soap bubbles, bounced off one another and wandered in every direction. The sharp jingle of the bells, sharp as the needles of frost glowing on the windowpane, rolled over the footpaths, roofs, and roads like ice balls the boys threw at pedestrians' feet.

"More! More!" shouted Walek when one of the boys fell down on his back. The others quickly covered him with snow—a huge snowdrift rose above him at once. They kept tearing off more white slabs, throwing them or laying them down if they were too heavy to throw. When their caps fell off, they stomped them into the snow, then shook them and put them back on, waiting for the lumps of snow to melt and trickle icily down their backs. The wind blew at their hair, threw snow in their eyes, flushed their faces.

Entering the tavern, Walek stumbled on a straw doormat and the whole place spun before his eyes. The doormat was frayed and creased, soaked with melted snow. The sour smell of fermenting wine, of beer tapped from the barrels, of vodka, and the nauseating smell of warmed-up bodies, sheepskin coats, leftover food—all those smells placed Walek in the world which he had watched through the little hole scratched in the windowpane. It was a world that he couldn't quite imagine.

Grandfather ordered a plate of sauerkraut stew ("Make sure the *bigos* is hot"). When Walek swallowed a few heaping spoonfuls, he felt his blood quicken in his feet and hands, and he wiped sweat drops off his forehead. The chunks of venison in the stew tasted different—did they?—from the venison and *bigos* cooked by his old aunt, Jadwiga, who was in charge of the Danilowskis' kitchen. And he, Walek, will never forget—because there are things, events, people that must never be forgotten—the taste of *bigos* eaten with rye bread, the meat carelessly chewed, the quickly cleaned plate. And he won't forget—because this mustn't be forgotten either—the taste of the first beer that he drank sitting in his grandfather's lap. Encouraged by the laughter of the amused patrons, Walek got away with his audacity because Grandfather pretended not to see what Walek was doing. After a few days when Grandfather told Walek's mother about it, she was shocked. In the name of God and in the name of Walek's love for her, she begged her son never to drink beer if he didn't want to see her dead. Walek promised he would never touch beer without her knowledge and permission.

A large spotted dog came out from under the table, raised its head, and started licking Walek's fingers. Behind the window, dusk was thickening, and the boys with whom Walek played could no longer be heard. Some patrons were going home, and others were taking their place. The faint light of kerosene lamps threw shadows on the walls. The smell of kerosene was spreading fast—faster than the darkness outside. The shadow of Rosenzweig, like the wings of a huge vulture, moved behind the counter, one time striking Walek with terror, another provoking him to mirth.

Attorney Danilowski has sucked the second mint on his way between Saint Augustine's Church and Orla Street. Evidently the time it takes to suck one mint is enough to pass the sacristy, Wendler's paint warehouse, Bat's shoe store, and then stop opposite Orla. If the attorney had put a third mint into his mouth and then a fourth one, he would have found himself on the stairs to his office. But maybe he has had enough sweets? Maybe so. The attorney stops in front of a barber shop and looks at his reflection in the window. He pulls up his collar and walks on.

Let us stop and look at the sky. In this account, intended as a detailed record of all events we witness, a chronicle of the events in the Book of the Day, we must not miss anything, not even the clouds. They too are preserved by our memory.

Describe the clouds? There are no clouds. There's no wind and there are no clouds. What can we see by staring persistently at the sky? A noisy flock of starlings flying from one cherry tree to another. If we are lucky, we may spot a hawk circling over the city.

Not even the slightest breeze moves the air. That doesn't mean, however, that the air is still. Quite the contrary. Honey-scented particles vibrate in the air, reminding us that the time of blooming and pollinating isn't over yet. In the diminutive gardens planted under the windows, the buzzing of bees alternately rises and falls. Life goes on.

Mrs. Zelda Baum walks out the door of her house, hesitates for a moment, not knowing whether to choose a shady or a sunny spot, and sits down on a bench in the sun. Insect wings flicker over the warm roof of the brewery. Mrs. Baum intently listens to their buzzing and watches the clouds of white, sour-smelling steam sliding down the brewery roof. She rolls up the sleeves of her dress and rests her palms on the edges of the bench. She closes her eyes. Nothing is happening.

Nothing is happening here—at the corner of Listopadowa and Lwowska. No smoke comes out of the pipe from the Baums' furnace. The cry of a hawk pierces the air; the third mint hasn't been put into the mouth; the steam slides down the roof.

Our statement that nothing is happening could be easily questioned by other observers. Let's add some new facts. Pigeons stroll on the roof of the Baums' shed. Mrs. Zelda Baum brushes the hair away from her forehead. Her eldest child spits out a piece of maggoty apple.

The grass near the brewery is wet, as if covered with dew. We're walking along the wall of the brewery down Listopadowa, leaving our footprints in the grass. The ashes from the Baums' furnace are gone. Soon our footprints will be gone. Let's stop while they are still visible. Future events will negate them.

Translation by Ewa Hryniewicz-Yarbrough

from

Castle Keep

William Eastlake

Just before the end of the world Captain Beckman gave us soldiers a lecture on the history of art. I mean, not too long before the Germans broke through in the Ardennes, here was a captain in the American Army telling us about the power, the force, of the Romanesque arch.

"What's that mean?"

"He's coming to it."

"On my time?"

"When there is no war," I whispered to de Vaca, "the higher-ups make sure the troops don't get an hour off. We might think, and if that happens we might win the war, spoil their game."

"Private Benjamin," Captain Beckman called from his lectern on top of a weapons carrier. "Private Benjamin, if you believe you are more qualified to give this lecture, if you want to do the talking, why don't you—"

"Thank you, sir. No, I'm sorry. Go ahead."

"Thank you, Private Benjamin," Captain Beckman said coldly. "Now, gentlemen, at this point I want to make clear that the Romanesque column should never be confused with the neo-classic patterns of the Renaissance, and there is another common esthetic pitfall that I want you to be aware of—art as early as the fifteenth century has raised the same question—always patterned upon the whimsical fantasy of the biological analogies. Gentlemen, there was no evolution from El Greco to Delacroix any more than there was any degeneration from Giorgione to Tiepolo. Empiric fallacies can be laid in part to the esthetic determinism that culminated in the industrial revolution."

"That thought could come in handy," Elk said.

Captain Beckman raised his arm. "Aren't we, gentlemen, faced with the same problem here as were the Pre-Raphaelites trying to struggle into the light without the guiding and figurative pulse of William Morris?"

"We know him well," Clearboy said.

"I am intrigued," Beckman said, "that we Americans can occupy this castle and imagine that we are living in an example of the neoclassic Renaissance. This is not true."

"Ain't so," de Vaca said.

"We can see it's not a valid premise if one notes the elliptical configurations capping the north tower. Do we see any esthetic or indeed any architectural anomalies in the north door?"

"Plenty."

"I want to suggest that there are no artistic anomalies, gentlemen, only preconceived progression in our own minds. What Rubens learned in Italy was not only reflected in his later painting but was, surprisingly enough, a revolutionary overlay that re-created rather than mimicked the Renaissance."

"It's difficult to believe, sir, isn't it?"

"Now, gentlemen, we are gathered here to fight a war, not to debate esthetic truths, but I suspect ten years from now, or twenty, at some American Legion convention, one of the nightmares you will have will be of that day in the Ardennes when you were not blown up by a bomb, a shell, but bored to death by Captain Beckman. But my purpose in this talk is to shock you, to make you realize by dull extension that there is a world completely unknown to you, without any reference to your imagined self, but I assure you it has tremendous implications to your true self. The function of art is to disturb and to awake. It's something that takes you apart and puts you back together again, a new person. All of you in the castle have the unique privilege of occupying a monumental tribute to man's concept of beauty."

"The hell you say, Captain."

"And if I can make some small analogy here to our present situation, I would like to suggest that war is not a science, no, not a science at all. War is an art. Does that seem a fair premise to you, Private Benjamin?"

"It certainly does, sir." And I thought, He's got his war to fight too. I should rescue him, but he's got to learn what this kind of combat means. He has taken on not only the whole American Army but the world. Jesus, you'd think he'd realize he can't get away with art in this man's army. He's liable to be arrested and shot, and I can see myself, the little black fellow on the end, the one with a grin on his face and the grenades around his neck, at the head of the firing squad.

"Do you concur, Private Benjamin?"

"I don't even know what that means," I said. And I thought, Sorry to let you down, sir, but you got to walk into this machine gun all by yourself.

"Corporal Clearboy," Captain Beckman continued bravely, "Corporal Clearboy, was it your estimate that your General Patton planned in advance his breakthrough out of Normandy?"

"I sure as hell don't know, sir."

"I wanted to hear you say that, Corporal Clearboy. I want to suggest here that there is the same spontaneity, the same revolution, not evolution, in war that there is in art. Corporal Clearboy was with General Patton, gentlemen, when the Seventh Army broke out of Normandy."

"But he and I were never close, sir."

"Nevertheless I think it makes my point about war being an art. Napoleon at Austerlitz, Hannibal at the Alps, Caesar at the Rubicon. You see, they couldn't have planned these victories. If you do the logical thing as a result of planning, that's what the enemy expects and they are ready for you. Both sides read the same books. War is an art of becoming, and I suspect that if art is not art—without art victory is an empty bauble. Let me make my statement clearly."

"You do that, sir."

"Science is an art. Let me read from my notes. Victory in war is best achieved by treating the processes of battle not as a science but an art. Would you agree with that compendium, Private Benjamin, as a tenable thesis?"

"What?" I said.

"Can you accept my premise?"

"I sure can, sir."

"Why?"

"Because I wasn't listening."

"This is supposed to be a training course. We don't have any training films up here, but Major Falconer wants us to keep the men occupied, so in my hour today I thought I'd kick around a pet theory of mine."

"Don't beat it to death."

"Which is . . ." Captain Beckman said, storming over objections.

"Science is an art," Clearboy said.

"No. War is an art. Think about it, gentlemen. The hypothesis first occurred to me through painting. Through the understanding of the problems of painting you begin to get a clue to the key to war. The painter heightens the perceptions of reality by ignoring reality. Let us say you are painting a picture of a mountain. The real mountain ceases to exist, but a mountain exists inside you. You are the heart of the mountain. In expressing that emotion in form and color, heightened reality perceptions are achieved and the viewer enters inside you through the mountain. Although your mountain is but an illusion, an emotion, I think the mountain emotion becomes. The art of becoming is a mutually shared perception with the artist. A culmination," Beckman said.

"An orgasm," I said.

"I want to say," Beckman said, "that the artist is not alone. He must share his involvement, his participation. The audience is his partner in an act of love. Yes, art is like a sexual experience, and a sexual experience, like art, cannot be culminated alone."

"Certain, sir?"

"Now, do you gentlemen remember the training film that Lieutenant Amberjack showed you?"

"The one on sex, sir?"

"Yes," Beckman said. "I would like to link that into the art of war, which that film didn't cover. Of course when you have a sex film you can't cover everything," Beckman said in a very weak joke. Nobody laughed. "Seriously, gentlemen, sex without love, like art without feeling, is nothing more than masturbation."

"Shall we put that down, sir?"

"No. I'm just throwing things out, gentlemen. I've got an hour to kill, and maybe I can give you something."

"Can we pursue that sexual thought further?" de Vaca asked.

"No. I want to speak about the art of war. I think I can make my point. My point is—"

"Yes, sir?"

"My point is . . . let me say my point was . . ."

"Yes, sir? Sex is an art?"

"No, Elk."

"Masturbation is an art?"

"No, de Vaca. I think the point is, and perhaps the whole point is, it's difficult to lecture for a whole hour without training films. But to get back to my point about war and women."

"War and art, sir."

"No, not now," Beckman said.

"I get your point," Clearboy said. "You don't plan an assault on a woman. You don't say, First I do this and then I do that. You don't worry about logistics, supplies, tactics, strategy. You just say, I'm going to climb that woman because that woman is there."

"That, gentlemen, is art. That, gentlemen, is war," de Vaca said.

"Have I made myself clear?" Beckman said, starting to leave.

"I'm afraid so, sir."

"Good. Are there any questions?"

"Yes, sir. What would you say if you heard your best girl was sleeping with a 4F?"

"I don't have to answer questions like that, Clearboy. My hour is up."

"Only twenty minutes, sir."

"Well, I'd say, Clearboy, screw that girl," Rossi said.

"But there's such a great distance, Sergeant."

"I want to get back to the war," Beckman said. "I want to leave you with a thought that might do you some good. I want to say to you bums that if you ever have to lecture a whole hour to a bunch of idiots, then resign your commission. If you have any more questions, see me in my office."

Everybody ran except me, Alistair Benjamin. I tracked Captain Beckman to his office.

"When I said 'See me in my office,' I didn't expect you to take me seriously, Alistair," Beckman said. "I want to be alone."

"You're a fun guy," I said. "Your talk turned me on."

"I don't want to be a fun guy," Captain Beckman said, sulking. "I didn't intend my talk to be a fun thing, but somewhere along the line I went wrong."

"No, it turned me on," I said. "Do you mind if I sit down?"

"No, you can stand," Captain Beckman said politely.

"I'm queer for art," I said. "Your long talk turned me on. All we get in the army is military crap. You rang a bell with what you said about painting."

"I'm a soldier," Beckman said defensively. "I see you sat down anyway. Privately, Private Benjamin, if people here hear us talking about these things, they'll think we're psychos. That is, that's the army. Anything out of the humdrum routine of killing people they can't accept. I had intended that lecture to be on the quick sketching of enemy terrain. If a soldier could bring back on paper an idea of what he saw, and not an exact drawing, it would mean more to him."

"But is war a subjective thing, sir?"

"That's a good point," Beckman said, taking out his pipe. "Are you comfortable?"

"Do you mean that facetiously?"

"I mean your being a private and my being a captain and everything."

"And everything?"

"Yes," Beckman said, loading his pipe while trying to load a question. "Don't you agree we can't discuss art while the enemy . . . while we're surrounded by the entire American Army?"

"I think you took your lecture too hard, sir. You should never underestimate the intelligence of American soldiers."

"Did you get that out of the training manual, Private Benjamin?"

"Yes, sir."

"Who do you suspect put it there?"

"Some klookhead."

"That's right," Captain Beckman said, igniting his pipe. His Zippo seemed loaded with TNT and lighted us in a big glare. "The two of us are secret sharers. We feel strongly about something that the army won't even admit exists."

"Art, sir?"

"We shouldn't use that word any more, Alistair," Captain Beckman said. "Even I find it difficult now in the context of soldiering—"

"You shouldn't be bitter, sir. After all, here we are in this perfect tenth-century castle surrounded by all these beautiful objects, rare authentic treasures. If a man did not appreciate them he would not be much of a man. If a soldier did not value them he would not be much of a soldier. Napoleon before Venice said, If my cannon destroy one statue, then I would rather not take Venice. That was a great soldier speaking, Captain."

"Did Napoleon say that, Alistair? It doesn't sound like Napoleon."

"No, Napoleon really didn't say that, sir. But I thought it would cheer you up."

"I appreciate that, Alistair. But Napoleon was a louse."

"Yes, sir."

"I think all soldiering is a bore, don't you? The plumed troops in the proud wars that make ambition virtue."

"Yes, sir. But I see you got a Purple Heart and the Silver Star."

"I got excited," Beckman said. "For a whole year I was out of my mind. But I've recovered now."

"But you'd fight for this castle, sir."

"Yes, but I don't know who," Beckman said, "I don't know which side, would want to destroy it."

"But you'd fight to preserve it."

"I don't know," Beckman said. "The only thing I'm certain of, absolutely sure of, is this: I may charge a machine gun, I may storm a fort packed with 88s, but, Alistair, I swear to you I'll never give another lecture."

"One thing more, sir."

"Yes, Alistair."

"I'm sorry I couldn't come to your aid during the lecture, Captain."

"That would have been beyond and above the call of duty."

"Still . . ."

"Not at all, Alistair. When you write your book, you can rescue me. No, don't bother. Just write well about this castle and how we kept it. That's not a bad title—Castle Keep."

"Thank you, sir."

"Not at all, Alistair. We are in this together. We have the same enemies, the same love. Even if we don't communicate, we understand."

"Yes, sir."

"Castle Keep."

"We will try, sir. Will that be all, Captain?"

"That is all."

from

Chinese Letter

Svetislav Basara

I

My name is Fritz. Yesterday I had a different name. Today my name is Fritz. I have nothing to say: I'm sitting in my room trying to type a hundred pages or so of my story. It seems nothing is happening. Yet, that's not true. Lots of things are going on: my heart is beating, my blood is circulating, my kidneys are somehow managing to purify my blood, the Earth is rotating (it almost makes me feel dizzy), and night is falling. There is some kind of incessant ticking in my head. My face is pulled over my skull; I have no idea what it looks like today, I just know that soon—if this ticking in my head doesn't stop—my face will collapse, like a crumpled plastic bag, and I'll go insane. This ticking feels like Morse code. I must be picking up the frequency of some radio station. I'll go insane if the ticking doesn't stop. I have a sense that I've become too big for myself: I feel as if I'm much smaller inside than the actual size of my body. I've just started writing, and already I have nothing to say. That's why I invent. But this isn't important: I was told to turn in about a hundred double-spaced pages and so I'll type until I'm finished. Nobody told me what I should write about. But they gave me a deadline. They said: "We'll come back soon." That was a long time ago, and look how little I've written. And what if I die, if I don't finish my story? Let's *call* it a story. Perhaps I'm already dead? No. The dead don't speak. I certainly know very little about myself, yet I know that I'm not dead. Perhaps I'll never die. That's not impossible: time goes by very slowly. Life goes much faster. I'm talking too much about myself. I better talk about something else. If this "else" exists. I'm not sure that I mentioned that time passes more slowly in the apartment building where I live than in other buildings. The tenant's association decided so. Therefore, what I am writing right now, I am still not writing. At best I'm writing the second or the third sentence of the introduction. And in the meantime so many things have happened: three-hundred-and-sixty heartbeats, about a hundred ticks in my head, the Earth has turned about a tenth of a degree. If that's the best way of describing such things. How's this possible? It looks like I'm pausing for a long time between some of the sentences. That seems to be what I'm doing.

.   .   .

How did this all start? I haven't started from the beginning. It looks like I don't know what's going on around me. Yesterday everything was different. I had some personal belongings: a book and some letters. I don't have them anymore. I only have illnesses. Actually—I have more of a memory of illnesses because I'm not in any pain right now. I have no doubt that illnesses are still working to destroy me but I don't feel anything. I haven't read the letters. It's a pity. I might have found out something more about myself. At least my address. But I regret most . . . I wanted to say: what I regret most is the book. I hadn't read the last few chapters. I never would've read them anyway.

.   .   .

Yesterday I had a hard time. I was going somewhere, I took the letters and the book with me, and I was walking around thinking how nice it would be if I didn't exist and at that moment somebody slapped me on the shoulder and shouted: "Well, well, well, look who's here!" At that very moment my pleasant daydreaming about non-existence dropped like a rock into a pool of water, creating a series of concentric circles—little waves that physics teachers use to illustrate how sound spreads through the air. I turned around and saw a very tall guy. I didn't know him. It was obvious that the man had made a mistake. He kept apologizing, he thought I was a friend of his, but I was not that friend. The day started off badly. I was going to visit a friend of mine. He had been lying in a hospital for months now and it was about time I paid him a visit. Everything that was happening seemed very suspicious. First of all, what kind of friend was he that, when I saw him in the hospital, it was the first time I ever saw him, yes, the first time in my life—this is what my friends are like. I sat down by his bed. Soldiers kept walking through the hospital room in camouflaged uniforms. Their barracks were somewhere nearby and I guess they were coming back from their duties. It might even be that they were coming back from war. It's possible: sprawled on a bed next to my (let's say) friend, there was a guy in a military shirt with a nasty wound in the chest. A hopeless case. And my friend was a hopeless case. And I was a hopeless case. And everyone, I now know, is a hopeless case. But I didn't know this yesterday.

.   .   .

The doctors were making all possible efforts to cure my friend so that he could die a healthy man. By the way: my father, on his death bed, used to say that for an honest man the best thing that can happen is to die healthy, surrounded by his family. Very idyllic, indeed. But, to make things even more confusing, the doctors themselves were hopeless cases. When things go wrong, nothing can stop them: that same day, at the same time, my friend was visited by his mother. But it was not his mother. I knew that because my friend was not paying any attention to her. I was sure she was somebody else's mother. Or at least a stepmother. My poor friend. He must have felt awful. He had a visit from a friend who is not his friend, and from a mother who is not his mother. Perhaps he was not he. I don't know how to explain this logically. I hate logic but sometimes I use it so that I won't die from anxiety. But even logic can't explain this: in the corner, on a bed without a bedspread, there was a marble statue of Julius Caesar. The passage of time had destroyed his nose, both ears, and left underarm. His skin was covered with a gray film and was cracking. (*Sic transit gloria mundi!*) Against all hospital rules there was a fresco of a woman on another bed—Simonida—with a blindfold across her eyes. I said to her kindly: "They gouged out your eyes, you pretty picture." She responded angrily: "Go to hell!" My friend's mother, who wasn't his real mother, said: "There, you see what children are like nowadays." I wanted to leave, but it wasn't easy to do so anymore: the doctor wouldn't let me.

.   .   .

"You have 3,300,000 red and 19,000 white blood cells," the white mask bending over my face was telling me. "Your blood test looks bad. The infection has gotten worse. An operation is the only choice we have." I was afraid of the operation. I didn't have any trust in a hospital where lost cases were treating other lost cases, even the ones who've been dead for a hundred years. I wanted to treat the infection with antibiotics, but the white mask was adamant: the operation was the only choice I had. I signed my consent form for the treatment and I don't know what happened to me after that. Perhaps I had an operation, perhaps I didn't have an operation, I might have died during the operation, I might not have died. If I had an operation it might have been only for my appendix. I already had every other operation. I was really afraid of appendix vermiformis. The infection could have easily caused an inflammation. In that case I would have to have an operation. What if the surgeon who was on duty that day happened to have a female acquaintance who was the relative of an idiot who lived in the same building in which an unimportant artist I couldn't stand also lived? What if the painter somehow found out that I couldn't stand him, and told the idiot that I hated him? Rumors spread very fast. The idiot might have said to his neighbor that I intended to kill the sculptor; the neighbor would sooner or later tell her relative that I killed the architect, and the relative—since she was the surgeon's cousin—would tell the surgeon all this in strictest confidence. Surgeons don't like killers of architects. What if that day that same surgeon was on duty? What if he left several pieces of gauze in my head *by accident*. If things took that turn, and who can tell that they didn't, my head is probably festering. Then it would be quite easy to cut my head off. For antiseptic reasons, let's say. Yes, yes, the ticks in my head. Perhaps they put somebody else inside me. Medicine can do wonders. And to complicate things further: dead or alive (as they say on wanted posters) I finally made it out of the hospital. Quite legally, I suppose. Nobody fired a gun at me. And my letters and my book were nowhere to be found. All right, I thought, letters come every day. Others will come. Even if I died, the letters would still come. Letters keep coming for a period of time after somebody dies. But the book? What happened to the book?

.   .   .

What could have happened to the book? I was thinking about that for about fifty meters, and then I couldn't walk any further. I had a wall in front of me. That's all I can say about the wall. My condition at that time could be described as: *it didn't matter that I stood in the rain*, but this isn't what I wanted to say. I just want to try to remember the last sixty seconds and the last fifty meters: I take a step forward, then I shift the weight of my body to my left leg and then I step to the right. We usually don't think about the mechanism of walking, but when you start thinking about it, the complexity of this mechanism hits you in the face and you are simply unable to take another step. I did this thirty times. Times two. Went to the wall. I could have done this differently. But I didn't. I looked stupid staring at the wall. I don't know how long I stayed in this position. I don't know how I got back home. It's really difficult to explain some things. So, I made my way back home and tried to think about everything. But it wasn't working. I'm trying even now. But it's not working. Still, something has passed. Five minutes have passed, for example. Finally, some more time has passed. That's because I'm thinking about the events from the past. It takes time for time to pass. I remember that I was overcome by enormous fear. I was afraid that my mother or sister or somebody else could walk into my room and ask me where I was. And as it usually happens, somebody (I won't say who it was) walked into my room and asked me where I'd been. I didn't know what to say. I forgot the script. I should have said that I had an operation.

.   .   .

An hour or two later, the two guys came. They said abruptly: "Write!" I asked, "What?" "Whatever you want." "How many pages?" "About a hundred!" Going away one of them paused at the door:
"We'll come back soon," he said.

II

Today my name is Fritz again. I have one problem: I exist. My biggest success in life is that I'm not dead yet. My biggest failure in life is exactly the same thing: I'm not dead yet. I was born and as a result I suffer all the consequences. If I exist, that's because I wanted to. I don't see any other possibility. I honestly envy those who don't exist. Those with no names and shape. Those who have no clue that they don't exist. But sooner or later they'll be drawn into the game too. Everybody succumbs in the end. If it weren't so, people would stop having children.

. . .

Existence itself isn't a big problem. The worst thing is my doubt about this existence. It often happens that I have gloomy thoughts and then I wonder: don't I exist only when this somehow fits my surroundings; isn't this the very reason that my name is on different lists and records? Am I not living on a street named after a person, and in a house with a number on it, so that these indicators would make it easier for other creatures to find my whereabouts? Let's not fool ourselves: the names of the streets aren't there to honor the dead but to track down the living. Once you've been born, they simply *force* you to live. To the degree they want, when the circumstances are convenient for them. You see, I'm persecuted: they force me to write. That's an old trick: everybody writes about persecution. But I have nothing against this state of affairs. It even pleases me. If they didn't persecute me, I'd be in a vacuum, left with nothingness and—what's worst—left with myself.

. . .

I've been thinking a little bit about what I see and feel and it all seems very suspicious. When I say this, I am thinking of myself and my surroundings. What gave me reason to be suspicious? Nothing! Simply nothing. These are the rules of the game: they persecute me so that they can convince me that I exist. I wish I could trust them. I insist on being persecuted. My retreat from the world should result in their asking: Where the hell is Fritz? They should start looking for me, and when they find me they should persecute me. Thank God, they found me. They ordered me to write. Perhaps they want my statement. All right! This is a part of my statement.

. . .

"The postman brought a letter for you," my mother says. A blue, official, registered letter that reads:
Note: the following mathematical problem should be solved.
If a traveler goes from place A to place B, and if the distance

between A and B is 86 km, and if he walks 5 km/h on average, how long will it take the traveler to get from place A to place B?

And, instead of a signature:

We'll come back soon!

.   .   .

That's just what I needed. Perhaps they know that I'm bad at math, so they want to make my job even harder. Where was I? Oh, yes. I have become submissive in my desire to be persecuted. For example, when in my rare walks I come across a policeman, I can hardly restrain myself from going up to him and saying: "I surrender! My name is Fritz! It's impossible that I'm not guilty. Take me with you!" However, I have never done this. Partly because of my cowardice, partly because of my *angular* way of looking at things. *Angularity*—that's my philosophy. I'm trying to observe all things by looking at them askance. The majority of people (those who see things at a 90 degree angle) see them as they are trying to appear. That's my view of looking at things when I'm crossing the street. This view is the safest in traffic. But life isn't made up of crossing busy streets, is it? Sometimes, you should look at things from an angular point of view. With this view you can't see anything except the misfortunes ahead. In spite of everything, I can't help but see things from an angular point of view, not even taking a peep at what's happening backstage, where you might see the destructive mechanism of deception. Let's take madness as an example. If somebody says that he's Alexander the Great, he'll be put into an insane asylum very soon. People have no problem with that. But there are lots of problems with doing this. I call myself by a different name each day; these days I call myself Fritz, and nobody says a word to me, nobody even thinks that I might be crazy. It's because Fritz is completely unimportant. But it's different with powerful people. The name Alexander the Great is important enough to instill fear in quiet, ordinary citizens and they do whatever is necessary to twist his noble plans, to intercept his visionary conquests that might crush their fragile—you could even call it "manufactured"—peace.

Translation by Ana Lucic

from

Chromos

Felipe Alfau

A family like that of Coello would be inconceivable except in two places: Spain, where they came from, and New York, where anything goes. This is not intended as a play on words but as a preparation for the incidents preceding the demolition of a building in Harlem, where this family lived, incidents which some members of the Spanish colony in that neighborhood considered incredible, while others considered highly significant and which, not having taken the trouble to doubt, I pass along to those enjoying the same lazy distaste for systematic disbelief.

The story might open on the day when Mr. Robinson called on the Coello family with the unselfish and civilizing purpose of illuminating the darkness in which this foreign family undoubtedly existed, of preaching to them some good modern sense, of rescuing them from their foolishness and of rendering them an invaluable service by, incidentally, selling to Don Hilarión Coello a life insurance policy.

Mr. Robinson did not know that day when he took derby, umbrella and briefcase and departed on his way to the Coellos, that his visit would be fateful and the starting point of events which he never suspected and never learned. He walked in one of those New York spring showers that last all week. As he crossed Lenox Avenue, the wind blowing caused him to lower his umbrella, blocking his view of traffic and he nearly walked in the path of a fast-moving taxicab and came close to putting an abrupt ending to many subsequent events. He heard the noise of brakes forcibly applied and of English forcibly used, all of which he disregarded with professional philosophy.

He turned into 123rd Street where Don Hilarión Coello lived.

The Coellos were a very proud and very mournful family. They lived in one of those apartments with an endless narrow corridor onto which small rooms open like cells and one cannot walk through without instinctively accelerating one's steps for fear that something may be lurking in one of the treacherous rooms, ready to spring, to snatch, as one passes.

If Don Hilarión called out authoritatively from one end of the house to his wife at the other end, she would have to journey that long corridor looking into every room repeating: "Where are you? where are you?" and she always grew a little afraid.

It was sad to look that way for a person, it was like one of those melancholy fairy tales or a dream, and yet it was an everyday affair.

That apartment, with all windows overlooking a court that was in itself a nightmare, could have turned the happiest person into the most helpless hypochondriac, let alone a family with the propensities of this one.

Black garment encased, somberly proud families like the Coellos, whose poverty has gone to their heads and are intoxicated with failure, were common in Spain and this was the paradox of the Coello family as of so many others. Unable as they would have been to remain themselves under changed conditions in a country of which they were a typical, if old product, they could be unmolested in New York and even contribute to its typically heterogeneous population. Here they could mourn the glad tidings about their country brought by the newspapers, they could wail and deplore to their hearts' content, remain in their pure unadulterated state, like calamares in their own black sauce, with all their militant, though aesthetically justified defensive chastity, worshiping traditions which dictate to cover the greatest possible area of human bodies. Don Hilarión Coello sported an abdomen like a balloon, and his wife one like an apron which would have permitted her to remain chaste even in a nudist camp.

As one of their friends said—an individual who having arrived here six months before them felt entitled to become their spiritual cicerone in the labyrinth of American life:

"That is the convenience of New York, Don Hilarión. On one side you have progressive Nordics who do gymnastics and read science, and on the other you have retrograde Latins who procreate behind shut windows and read the catechism."

"You have said it." Don Hilarión spoke with a very profound and important manner: "On one side you have one thing and on the other you have the other thing. On one side the wrong and on the other the right."

Don Hilarión felt very important, and his family thought that he was and therefore they also felt very important. Don Hilarión was a notario, not a notary, mind you; that does not quite convey the meaning, but a notario. A notario in Spain, at least in Don Hilarión's day, was a title given to a man having achieved the summit of his career in the field of law. It was the coronation of every law student. When parents addressed good children showing particular brilliance, they always said: "Study law, my boy. It has many applications, among them the diplomatic service, and you may even someday be a notario and always be respected and looked upon as an important citizen, not to speak of the good profits you will derive." And the good children always imagined themselves with beard, silk hat and a frock coat, walking along the street acknowledging the deferential greetings and respectful salutations of the admiring crowds.

Don Hilarión had been one of those boys.

He had studied law.

He did not enter the diplomatic service because he only had studied two dead languages.

He did not wear a silk hat and a frock coat, because his friend and spiritual guide had advised him that in this country one did not have to be ceremonious, but do as one pleased; a somewhat exaggerated statement, but safe where Don Hilarión was concerned.

He did not have any greetings to acknowledge, except occasionally those of the janitor and of one or two acquaintances, because the rest of the population did not know him from Adam.

But Don Hilarión was a notario. He felt important. His family felt important. But they were Spaniards of the old school and therefore were gloomy.

Their obvious reason was that Don Hilarión could not practice law in New York because he was not a citizen and besides, his knowledge of English was very limited. However, he had set up one of his rooms as an office, with all his law books, solid cabinets, large imposing desk and heavy chairs. The room was small, Don Hilarión fat, and consequently it was difficult to move about the place. Once he succeeded in sitting at the chair behind his desk, it was not easy to induce him to abandon his post and leave the room, and Don Hilarión sat there all day, reading newspapers from Spain, and it made him feel like a very busy man. This room was at the end of the long corridor and it was from there that Don Hilarión, finding it difficult to extricate himself, called out to his wife who was most of the time with Vicenta, the servant, in the kitchen, unfortunately located at the other end, and she had to look in every one of the rooms, when she very well knew that he could be but in one, held there at the mercy of his furniture.

Doña Dolores arrived breathless: "What is it, Hilarión?"

"Nothing, woman, what can it be? The usual thing. Can you lend a hand? I want to get out of here and I am in a hurry. Where did you think I was?"

By this time she had already got hold of his hand, heaved and given him a good start. "That's enough now, woman. I can manage the rest by myself."

"Such small rooms in this country! In Spain this furniture was lost in that office you had, remember?" Her voice was very throaty, very weepy.

"No use complaining, woman. Nothing gained by that," Don Hilarión finished, heading for the bathroom, newspaper in hand.

Doña Dolores walked back swiftly along the corridor wailing at her memories, at her wretched present: "Those were rooms! At least one had that in one's poverty." She assumed a very resigned air, very browbeaten. "But when one is so poor one does not even have the right to complain . . ." She reentered the kitchen and ably turned her lingering remarks into a fitting continuation and confirmation of her interrupted talk with Vicenta:

"I should say one has no right to complain. With sufferings, one finally does not mind anymore. But still there are things that reach your marrow. Don't think I don't notice, Vicenta. I did not want to say anything the other day about the incident of the shoes of Hilarión—but the procession goes on inside."

She referred to her husband having had a patch placed on one of his shoes. Then he had met some friends and they had walked. One of them was a Spanish writer who wrote chronicles about New York for South American papers and was always making bad suggestions. This time he suggested that they all examine their feet, right where they were, on Seventh Avenue, to determine who had the largest.

Don Hilarión suspected that the writer had spied his repaired shoes and was calling attention very indelicately to the fact. He had arrived home feeling very depressed and had discussed the incident with his wife in front of Vicenta. The matter had gradually diminished in his mind, but in Doña Dolores's it had behaved like a rolling snowball, reaching the phenomenal proportions of a unanimous world confabulation to vex them, to mock their honorable poverty.

Vicenta tried to soothe her with the usual speech: "Don't think about it, Doña Dolores. A writer! Like all the rest of them. They are always talking for the sake of talking. Who takes writers seriously?"

But Doña Dolores persisted. She relished such experiences that made her feel like a martyr. She resented Vicenta's lightly discarding the matter, simply because she had no appearances to maintain, robbing this succulent humiliating morsel of all its imagined seasoning. She skillfully misinterpreted:

"All right, Vicenca, you let it go at that. It does not hurt you. When one is poor, one does not even have the privilege of complaining. Being poor is the worst sin I suppose, which must be constantly expiated, paid for, when one can pay for nothing else." She compressed her lips and a wistful smile sent her eyes in search of remote places of mournful reveries.

Vicenta, whose salary had not been attended to for the last six months, misunderstood sincerely: "Doña Dolores, you know very well that I am not one to think of certain things and I am very happy to work for you as it is. But what you do is like someone stabbing you and then you take the knife and twist it around."

"Now I twist it around! When one is in my position, one must be even accused, held to blame for one's own sufferings." She shifted to the other section of her servant's speech which offered opportunities too tempting to pass over: "And as for the other matter, Vicenta, you will be paid. Don't worry." Her voice rose to eloquent heights: "you will be paid even if I have to tear the flesh off my bones like that famous merchant of Italy, and you can have the blood too."

"Please! Doña Dolores! I am not worrying—" Vicenta gave up in hopelessness and turned to proceed with her chores and made an attempt at changing the conversation: "What shall we order from the grocer's today?"

"Anything," said Doña Dolores, disgusted with her servant's reluctance to continue her pet type of talk. "You know better than I. That is, if they want to send it. We also owe them money and—"

An interruption was advancing tumultuously along the corridor and invaded the kitchen. It was her two children, a boy and a girl, Jeremias and Angustias, both thin, sallow-complexioned and darkly sad-eyed. Both spoke with the same tearful throatiness of their mother and showed already strong-inherited and well-encouraged tendencies to gloom, contrasting with their noisy if not cheerful behavior. This last strange and unexpectedly inconvenient attitude for Doña Dolores was resignedly explained in her mind by what she considered the vulgarizing influence of the environment. Superficially, both children had become thoroughly Americanized in an amazingly short time. They were even called Jerry and Angie in school, a thing which extracted most devilishly from their names all the glorious, tragic implications.

"We want lunch!" Jerry shouted brutally, but with elegiac overtones.

"And in a hurry!" Angie completed with even worse manners and heart-rending harmonics.

Their mother withered them with a well-planted look: "I don't know what has come over these children since we came to this country. They were never like this in Spain. They have changed so!" In Spain they were half their present age, and never left home.

The children had sat at the kitchen table with drooping mouths and heads humbly to one side, to eat the lunch that Vicenta was preparing for them.

"Mama, can we have some money for carfare?"

"Yes, teacher is taking us to the Museum of Natural History and each one is supposed to provide his own carfare."

"Now you want money for carfare. When it is not one thing, it is the other. In that school they are constantly demanding money. We are poor and can't afford it."

"Oh, Mama! All the other children are going. Must we always be thus humiliated before others?" Their chins quivered, their voices shook effectively.

"Yes, I know. You have begun to suffer privations early, but you must be resigned. Being poor is no shame when one is honest. You go back to school and tell that teacher that your father cannot afford these luxuries like the rich parents of other children, but that you don't mind, that your father is a respectable notario and that in our poverty we base our pride." Her voice was decidedly damp.

"But Mama, you know they won't understand all that." They appeared to have given up melancholic displays as useless.

"Well, they should. It is high time someone woke them up to

the fact that this life is not a novel. In this country they have no consideration. All they think of is money and good times, always telling one to be gay and keep smiling." She made an effective pause. "Smiling! Yes, while the procession goes on inside. These women teachers here never marry, never have children, they don't know what suffering is, what privation, what life is."

"All right, Mama, but can we have the money?"

"Go on now," Vicenta stepped in: "You have enough museum pieces with those bespectacled old hens who teach you—"

"Miss Finch is not an old hen and she does not wear spectacles," Angie charged.

"Never mind that. You go back there and tell them that you did not get the money. Come on! Finish that omelet. You have appetites like millionaires. We can't be throwing food away in this house. Your father—" Vicenta checked herself. This pessimism was contagious. "Go ahead now, hurry! Run along and take an umbrella. It is raining."

And so it was and at this time, under another umbrella, Mr. Robinson was fatefully walking toward their house.

No sooner had the children left than Doña Dolores resumed her interrupted litany: "I suppose I should also laugh at the question of the cream puffs. I should be very cheerful about it."

"There you go talking about that again," Vicenta said while looking into the icebox and kitchen closets to see what was needed. She knew the incident by memory. For some reason it was one of the selected tear-jerking, bitter-smile-squeezer pieces in Doña Dolores's repertoire.

It seems that a friend, knowing Don Hilarión's precarious financial condition, had given him some matter to investigate concerning Spanish law. It turned out to be a very simple matter and Don Hilarión felt that it detracted from his importance as a notario to do a piece of work that could have been attended to by any law apprentice, any law office amanuensis. However, when he was paid, he made his grand gesture. He went to a pastry shop run by another Spaniard in the neighborhood and bought some cream puffs.

"To sweeten the bitterness left by this humiliating job," he said as he laid them on the table before his wife.

That night they had dinner accompanied by the usual lamentations all around. When time for dessert arrived, the children greeted the appearance of the cream puffs with vociferous sadness.

"You must be grateful for this little luxury, my dears. It has cost your father very trying moments, but do not be common. Poverty is no excuse for bad manners."

Angie was the first one to make the nefarious discovery. She held up the puff she had opened, under the overhanging lamp, for all to see: "This pastry is bad. Look, it is green inside."

Doña Dolores looked, they all looked. Vicenta had appeared at the dining-room door and also looked. This was a real crisis and Doña Dolores rose to it:

"Rotten!" she exclaimed in piercing tones. "Even that! Poor people must be given rotten things, because they have no money to buy at the right places—" She was beside herself. "That is too much. We may be poor, but too proud to permit such insolence!" The children's mouths were already drooping and trembling at the corners. "Take them back immediately, Hilarión!" Angie began to bawl shamelessly, a true Desdemona, and her brother bit his lip and cast his eyes down, a little man in distress. Doña Dolores fell prone upon the table, wiping aside the guilty puff: "Mockery, Hilarión—rotten mockery!" she wailed prostrate by the shock.

Vicenta surveyed the scene in perplexity. Don Hilarión gathered the offending puffs back into their box of shame and left like one walking to his doom, muttering between his teeth: "How long, my Lord, how long?" He returned the pastry, got his money back, and bought himself some cigars instead.

That incident had been one of the high, cherished moments of the Coello family.

"Just when poor Hilarión, happy at having earned some money, wanted to celebrate by giving his children something sweet, which they so seldom have." Doña Dolores concluded: "I am supposed to dance a fandango for sheer happiness."

At that moment the doorbell rang. Mr. Robinson had arrived.

Vicenta walked the length of the corridor wiping her hands on her apron and opened the door. Mr. Robinson introduced himself and in that roundabout manner which every salesman considers deceptive and enticing, he hinted at the purpose of his call. Such linguistic subtleties were beyond Vicenta's neglected knowledge of English and she called her mistress:

"Doña Dolores, please come and see what this man wants."

Doña Dolores was slightly more successful than her servant and understanding that the man had something good for her husband, she led Mr. Robinson, who had not removed his derby, into her husband's office: "Hilarión, this gentleman has come to see you."

Don Hilarión removed his gold-rimmed spectacles and regarded the gentleman. He assumed his most important manner, meanwhile trying to rise unsuccessfully: "Please have a seat, sir. In what can I serve you? Forgive me for not rising, but as you see, this furniture—"

"Don't bother. It's perfectly all right," said Mr. Robinson, squeezing past some furniture and into a chair. "My name is Robinson of the ——" he gave the name of some insurance company, and with that he opened his briefcase and spread his subject's literature before the prospective client, right over the newspaper that the latter was reading. Then in a speech not too short to be unimpressive and not too long to be wearisome, he stated his case, being careful to make himself clear to this foreigner.

Don Hilarión and his wife, who stood in the doorway, listened, the former pompously, the latter politely. Then when Don Hilarión thought naively enough that Mr. Robinson had finished, he cleared his throat and began: "You see, Mr. Robinson, I do not believe in life insurance policies, I—"

The other took ready advantage of Don Hilarión's halting English to lunge confidently onto well-trod ground: "What do you mean you don't believe? I don't care how rich you are. No one can afford to be without this protection. What about your wife, your children? Suppose you die one of these days. If you have the policy I have been speaking of, your wife won't have the added expense of your funeral, and she will get some money besides—"

"Holy Virgin!" Doña Dolores cried on the verge of a faint. "Listen to what this man is saying. He is talking about your death, and he dares suggest that I profit by it." Her face had gone from pallor to deep red. "Listen, mister. We may be poor, but we are no ghouls and when anyone dies in this family, God forbid, we shall obtain the money somehow to give them a decent, Christian burial. Listen to him!"

"Please, woman! Let me bear this cross alone," Don Hilarión said, while Mr. Robinson looked from one to the other endeavoring to make out these foreigners. "Pardon, Mr. Robinson, but as I said before, I do not believe in life insurance. No one can insure his life. One never knows when one will die and therefore there is no use—"

"Listen, brother. You don't know what you are talking about. If you would let me explain—"

Don Hilarión had succeeded in rising: "I don't know what I am talking about? Did you say I don't know what I am talking about?" He smiled a superior smile and deliberately placed his gold-rimmed spectacles upon his nose. "Perhaps you don't know whom you are talking to, sir. I happen to be a notario. Do you hear? A notario."

"So what? What's so wonderful about that? I am a notary also, and I can prove it."

There was a silence. Doña Dolores approached, Don Hilarión removed his glasses and leaning on his desk scrutinized his visitor, hat and all.

"You are also a notario?"

"Sure! What's wrong with it? Anybody can be one. All you do is pay a few dollars and you are a notary."

Don Hilarión staggered and, holding on to the arms of his chair, he slid down into his seat slowly, dejectedly, like one crushed to dust that settles gradually. Another silence followed, a longer one, like the kind that comes after an explosion.

"For a few dollars—anybody—a notario—" he managed to whisper hoarsely.

Doña Dolores precipitated herself forward and reached across the desk, a hand gripping her husband's shoulder: "Hilarión, Hilarión! Oh my God!"

"What did I do now?" questioned Mr. Robinson, puzzled. These foreigners were too much for him.

"What have you done?" Doña Dolores had turned on him like a lioness: "You have killed him!"

"But madam, I only—"

"Go away, please. Can't you see that he is ill? Go away!"

"All right, lady." Mr. Robinson picked up all his papers. "I'll be back when he is feeling better." He walked out hurriedly despite the furniture. He had nearly sold his best policy to a man who could die at the slightest provocation.

Doña Dolores was hovering over her fallen husband: "What is it, Hilarión? Speak to me."

Don Hilarión heaved a sigh that was like lifting a ton of bricks: "Nothing, woman, nothing—I prefer not to speak now," and then he began to talk. That man usually of so few chosen words began to talk rapidly, carelessly, in a manner his wife had never heard before. He poured out his soul. He spoke of his life, a subject he had always skipped with dignified reticence. He spoke of his hopes and illusions, of his disappointments and subsequent pessimism.

"Forgive me," he ended. "I have been talking a good deal and one should not burden a woman with one's troubles, but sometimes a man talks as he swims: to save himself from drowning. Talking is for the soul what motion is for the body. The body moves, does; the soul speaks, explains. I had to talk, but now I have to rest. I feel very tired. You go about your things and let me rest awhile." And Don Hilarión leaned his head on a hand that also shielded eyes no longer adorned with gold-rimmed spectacles.

"My poor Hilarión! What a blow!" said Doña Dolores, or rather, her lips formed the phrase silently, and silently she left the room, and once in the corridor she walked with more resolution to the kitchen.

Don Hilarión remained in the same position for a few moments. Then his eyes opened and he noticed once again the Spanish paper he had been reading. In sudden rage, he crumpled it up into a shapeless ball and hurled it against the walls lined with his law books. Then he sat back, his breath coming in gasps, and his eyes roved over those books. For only a few dollars anybody could be a notario!

He felt an uncontrollable desire to tear those volumes from the shelves where they reposed, to trample them, to smash them. He made an effort to rise and something snapped inside of him sending a sharp pain from his chest along his arms. Everything reeled, everything went dark: "Dolores—Dolores—!" he cried with despair.

Doña Dolores was rushing along the long corridor, looking into every room: "Where are you? Where are you?" She finally reached his room: "Hilarión, what is it, Hilarión?"

Don Hilarión did not answer. He was leaning back in his chair, his head drooping on one shoulder, his arms hanging lifelessly down the sides.

"Hilarión, are you sick? Hilarión, speak! Hilarión—! Vicenta! Come!" she howled.

Don Hilarión was dead.

To try to convey in words the extremes to which Doña Dolores went in displaying her just, unquestionable sorrow, would be impossible and if possible, useless, since no one could conceive of it more than of the stellar light-years in a book of astronomy. One can conceive possibly the feelings of a panhandler who is seeking five cents for a cup of coffee and suddenly finds himself owning the treasures of Ali Baba, then one could raise that to the nth power, but it would do no good. One cannot conceive that, and yet this is but like an orange compared to the earth if one considers the sorrow of Doña Dolores, the full measure of her bereavement.

Even she felt that it was quite impossible to do complete justice to her position, and like a clever actor fearing that a role may lie beyond his dramatizing potentialities, she wisely and conveniently for the surrounding world chose to underact her part. In all her sympathy-acknowledging answers she was sober and introduced simple phrases such as: "No, nothing, my dear. He left us nothing but his good name and the honor of bearing it," and "Yes, my dear, quite unexpected, but those who live honestly in spite of their poverty are always ready when the moment arrives," or "That is right, my dear. Death is the common leveler and no amount of money can pave the road to the kingdom of heaven and it is easier for a camel to pass through the eye of a needle—" But her expression was a thing to behold and she always ended with the same words: "Ay! They did not baptize me Dolores for nothing!"

But throughout all this Doña Dolores smiled wisely, sadly and to herself, as one who is keeping a secret. She was preparing her great coup, her fitting and masterly stroke. When words failed, it was time for action, and since tears, sobbing, nervous attacks and bellowing could do no justice to the situation, she, Doña Dolores, the champion mourner, would not be caught napping. She would do something, she would do something that would show how she could feel such a thing, something that would break all previous records set by the loudest mourners in this world, something memorable that would put to shame the most rabidly unfortunate characters in history.

Two days after the death of Don Hilarión, Doña Dolores summoned a Spanish undertaker by the name of Zacatecas. They remained a long time closeted in Don Hilarión's office, where the body lay in state. When they came out, enigmatic phrases were heard:

"You must reconsider the price, Señor Zacatecas. We are poor. He left us nothing but his good name and—"

"I know, madam, but this is a special job and besides, I may get into trouble and the least that could happen would be losing my license. Also remember that you would have had to buy a coffin."

"Very well, Señor Zacatecas. Please hurry and do your best."

"Oh, don't you worry about that. I will do my best. Now I am going for lunch and to my office to get some things and will be right back."

The Señor Zacatecas having left, Doña Dolores walked up and down the corridor several times, an unfathomable and resolute smile upon her lips.

When the Señor Zacatecas returned as promised with a large black case, she ushered him again into her husband's office and left him there behind the closed door. After that she had to perform what she called the painful duty of taking some nourishment to remain alive for the children's sake and then she sat surrounded by friends and acquaintances like a queen on a throne to bask in their admiring sympathy and discuss and comment at length with undisputed authority upon the exemplary past actions and never well-praised virtues of the illustrious and important defunct, while some black-attired guest summed up matters with a deep remark such as: "The real trouble with life is death."

Time passed and a few close and dejected friends sat at her sadly regal, if materially poor table to "do something for life, since one can do nothing for death" by eating a hasty supper prepared and served by Vicenta with red swollen eyes and unsteady hands.

The children sat through all this together, their thin faces paler than ever, Angie crying intermittently under the protective arm of her brother.

"Vicenta, please see that the children eat something."

"Yes—Doña Dolores," she said shakily and she went to the children and, holding them tightly with trembling arms, she disappeared with them into the kitchen, sobbing.

The mournful gathering remained repeating the same words, singing the same praises until well into the night. The children also remained up, Doña Dolores affecting an adequate disregard for anything not connected with her bereavement.

And then the Señor Zacatecas emerged from Don Hilarión's office where he had been all that time and called Doña Dolores, who responded immediately, reentering the room with him.

They remained there mysteriously with door closed quite a while and then she reappeared, followed by the Señor Zacatecas and closing the door carefully behind. Then she summoned everybody.

All the guests walked in single file along the corridor, Vicenta and the children bringing up the rear. They arrived as the Señor Zacatecas was taking his leave noiselessly like a shadow, and standing in front of the closed room, they met Doña Dolores, arms folded, beaming upon them her despair, her tragedy:

"I have summoned you all to witness the proof of my devotion." She quoted the old saying cryptically: "Things you will see of the Cid, that will cause the stones to speak." And she flung the door open.

The grief-stricken gathering crowded in the doorway and gasped.

Don Hilarión was sitting at his desk, in typical pose, pen in hand resting on a sheet of foolscap, his gold-rimmed spectacles balanced on his nose. There was even a frown clouding his noble brow as if it were laden with the problems and responsibilities of justice. The Señor Zacatecas had done a good job.

The wall behind his chair displayed a Spanish flag, adding to the sad arrangement a touch of glorious brilliance. It was a perfect picture of dignity, sacrifice and important futility. Doña Dolores had risen to unsuspected heights of genius to meet the challenge of the occasion:

"From now on," she said throatily but with appropriate self-control and an edge of fatigue in her voice, "this will be his shrine, his sanctuary. He will sit among his legal books and papers, in the atmosphere that was his life." She grew stern with the assurance of the cruelly wounded person before an appreciative, almost envious audience: "They shall not take him away from me. He was our only and most precious possession in our poverty. He was all we had. His exemplary life, his important achievements, no longer appreciated in these materialistic days, shall guide us in our dark hours of sorrow. He was a notario as you all know and he will remain one. Indeed death is the common leveler and all dead notarios are equal. In the new fields he is conquering, his well-justified ignorance of a vulgarly modern language will no longer stand in his path to glory. Here you behold Don Hilarión Coello, Notario."

"Doña Dolores—" came from every mouth like a murmur in response to her funeral oration. It sounded like "ora pro nobis," and involved an admiring recognition that was worth living for. The children hung on to Vicenta's apron, their faces a deathly white, their eyes like saucers. Doña Dolores raised a hand in the classic mob-stilling gesture:

"I propose to pay him homage once a year on the anniversary of his departure. He shall remain here, where he can be respected and honored as he deserves, but I appeal to your honorable sense of secrecy to keep this from misunderstanding outsiders as it would be very sad to have him who was a respected and important man of law involved in legal complications." There was a strange leer on her face as she lighted two candles which had been placed on the desk and knelt in front of it.

"Doña Dolores—" The murmur rose again, and again it sounded like "ora pro nobis," which smoothly turned to general prayer trailing among the kneeling figures along the corridor. Then Doña Dolores rose, and all, knowing that the audience was over, filed out silently, still crossing themselves with reverent fear.

When they had all departed, Doña Dolores put out the candles and locked the door of the shrine. Vicenta was standing in front of her, the children still grasping her apron. They looked like a petrified group and Vicenta said hollowly:

"I wouldn't do that, Doña Dolores. It does not seem right."

"Let anyone try and take him away," Doña Dolores responded with threatening finality as she pocketed the key.

The next two days Doña Dolores spent several hours enclosed with her dead husband. On the third day she only stayed a few minutes and when she came out she telephoned the Señor Zacatecas to come immediately.

As soon as he arrived she took him into the room: "Look here, Señor Zacatecas. There seems to be something wrong with your work. There is a strong smell and then also stains in the face and hands. I have not looked further because I did not want to disarrange anything until you got here. Come and look for yourself. Don't you notice the smell?"

They struggled past the furniture. The Señor Zacatecas bent close to the figure, he looked, he sniffed, he finally straightened up: "That cannot be helped, Madame, the job is good. I worked for hours on him. If you had called me sooner it would have been easier, but when you called me, he was already in pretty bad shape and it was hard work to get him in the position you see him now. I had to use special chemicals and after a while they react that way. But this is nothing. You keep the windows open for a while and it will wear off. I really don't want to know any more about this affair. I may get in trouble. I only did it because we are both Spanish and must stand together, but I want no more of it." The Señor Zacatecas departed.

Doña Dolores opened the window and looked into the pallid abyss of the court. Her gaze then remained suspended in space for a long time and then she also left the room.

That first year went by slowly at first and then it gathered speed uneventfully. In the beginning Doña Dolores's visits to her husband were frequent and the children lived in constant fear, stayed away from the house as much as possible and at night insisted that Vicenta sleep with them. Then after a few months the visits of Doña Dolores grew more scarce. She seemed to prefer to pour her eternal lamentations enriched by this magnificent new addition into the faithful, though inattentive ears of her servant. Then a few days before the anniversary, it was decided to pay a call on Don Hilarión to see that everything was as it should be.

They discovered that all the furniture had accumulated an alarming amount of dust, as had Don Hilarión. They considered the matter at length and finally arrived at the conclusion that everything had to be dusted, including the old notario.

"I thought it might be disrespectful," said Vicenta, "but what can one do?"

"It is more respectful to clean him, to perform that duty instead of allowing him to accumulate dirt. After all, Vicenta, cleanliness is next to holiness."

They left the room and Vicenta returned to it with duster and broom. She swept the floor as well as the furniture permitted and then dusted every piece with expert hand. When she came to Don Hilarión, she remained a while, duster in hand poised in midair, and then with a shrug of the shoulders, she began vigorously.

At the first stroke the duster caught the gold-rimmed spectacles and sent them crashing against the desk, one of the lenses breaking.

"Now I've done it!" poor Vicenta said in distress. She picked up the spectacles and with some effort she managed to balance them upon Don Hilarión's nose, which seemed to have shrunk. Indeed, the whole figure appeared slightly shrunk and distorted out of position, and then she also noticed Don Hilarión's face. It had also changed, for it seems that time passes even for the dead. His lips had receded somewhat and began to expose his teeth, with the suggestion of a macabre smile. The frown in his forehead was a bit accentuated. The whole face and hands looked much darker. Vicenta studied the whole thing for a while shaking her head and then left the room closing the door.

When the anniversary arrived Doña Dolores invited a few friends. They arrived endeavoring to cover their curiosity with an air of great reverence and when Doña Dolores opened the door of the sanctuary, they all crowded in with almost abject hurry.

Doña Dolores was about to deliver the speech she had prepared for the occasion when she caught sight as well as all the others of the expression on her late husband's face. The lips now fully exposed the teeth in a decided broad smile and the frown had become marked to the point of ferocity. The contrast was, to say the least, disconcerting.

Doña Dolores approached the sitting figure and eyed it. She overheard snickers and giggles and even a remark or two from a couple of American guests about the skeleton in the family closet. They all seemed nervous, fidgety. A young lady became hysterical.

And then Doña Dolores's eye fell upon the broken spectacles: "What is the meaning of this? Vicenta, come here. Explain!"

The dejected servant advanced twisting her apron in embarrassment: "Well, madam, the duster caught on the spectacles and they fell and—" She broke down and rushed from the room crying, her apron already a sausage in her hands, to seek refuge in the kitchen.

Doña Dolores looked at her husband's face again and mused: "I wonder what chemicals that Zacatecas used?"

The guests seemed unable to restrain their risibilities. Their rampant fear had created a nervousness which found only this outlet. They gulped, inflated their cheeks, coughed applying their handkerchiefs to their faces, and grew purple.

Doña Dolores turned upon them, the livid image of righteous indignation: "Shooo, imbeciles!" she emitted with all her might.

And this was too much for the guests. With howls and roars, they stampeded out of the house, convulsed by loud, open, ribald laughter.

The ceremony had ended.

The second year went by even faster than the first. The family activities had progressively invaded the room. There were things there which had to be used. At first Doña Dolores or Vicenta entered on tiptoe and left silently, but later they hurried and forgot to close the door on their way out and the door was open most of the time. The children appeared to have lost their fear. They played in the corridor and once when their ball rolled into Don Hilarión's office, Jerry walked in boldy, retrieved it, and as he was leaving, he stopped to study his father.

"Come over here," he called to his sister and when she came: "'S funny, but doesn't he remind you of someone, with that mustache and all?"

Angie looked carefully, her head to one side: "That's right! That portrait in the principal's office in the school."

"Doesn't it though?" They both laughed and then, forgetting all about it, resumed their play right in there.

Doña Dolores, who saw them as she came in from shopping, scolded them that time, but the scene was repeated often later and she minded it less each time and eventually noticed it no more. She was going through that critical age in which women sometimes become slightly stupefied.

Vicenta dusted Don Hilarión regularly like another piece of furniture. Once while thus occupied, she noticed that the pen had fallen from his hand. She tried to replace it but the fingers had contracted or separated and wouldn't hold it. She tried to press them together and one of them came off in her hand. Vicenta contemplated this minor disaster stoically. She remained undecided with the finger in her hand looking for an adequate place to deposit the relic. At last she dropped it in the wastebasket. When Doña Dolores eventually spotted the missing finger, she simply sighed and said: "That Zacatecas—that Vicenta—!"

More time passed and one day when Doña Dolores had to use the desk, she discovered that her husband was in the way: "Come over, Vicenta, help me with this."

Together they shoved Don Hilarión and chair and when Doña Dolores finished whatever she had to do at the desk, they forgot to replace the throne and master, and he remained in that position, on the side of the desk, like one applying for something to an invisible provider.

The family moved and lived about that corpse as if it were but an object, one more useless object which Vicenta had to attend to protestingly. One could often see Doña Dolores sitting there writing a letter or one of the children doing homework, with the vigilant, immobile figure next to them, frown, spectacles, mustache, smile, teeth and all.

The third anniversary passed unnoticed and when Doña Dolores remembered, she realized that it would have been an anticlimax to open a door which had been open already for such a long time. Besides, her friends were already completely familiarized with the presence of Don Hilarión. He had been very often included in their visits and two friends left the house once talking like this:

"But how is it that the authorities have not found out about this irregularity? Or if they have found out, why have they done nothing?"

"Well, you know. These foreign families can live in New York in their own colony, completely isolated from the rest of the town, like in an independent state. As long as they do not bother the rest, the city does not bother to find out. The thing remains among the group, but if anyone outside their circle has learned of it, it has been probably discarded as an old Spanish custom."

This explanation was as good as any, and as for the children, they were entering that age in which they felt ashamed of being connected with anything different from the rest and they did not mention it. Perhaps they did not give it enough importance anymore.

Don Hilarión was still holding together in spots, but on the whole, he looked quite bad and threatened to disintegrate completely at any moment. Every time he was moved, one could feel something snap, crush and roll down to accumulate in the folds of his clothes, in small particles, like crumbled fragments of old cork that sometimes found their way to the floor and had to be swept up.

One day Vicenta said to her mistress: "You know, Doña Dolores? This thing is falling apart, and it is only in the way here. I think we could put it in a trunk and send it down to the basement. Then we will have more room and we certainly need it with all this heavy furniture."

Doña Dolores pursed her lips and looked her husband up and down: "Yes—I suppose so. The purpose would be the same. I only promised not to let them take him away, and I am a woman of my word, but I suppose he will be better off that way."

And Don Hilarión, in the collapsible condition he had reached, was easily crammed into a trunk and sent down to the basement.

Time moved on to the melancholy accompaniment of Doña Dolores's lamentations, seasons followed seasons, and years pursued years with gradual acceleration, and the story might close one day when Mr. Goldstein, the landlord, called on the Coellos, thus saving them from perishing under the ruins of the building which had to be demolished, and incidentally to render them the service of another apartment in another building which he also owned. Mr. Goldstein did not know that day, when disregarding coat and hat he left his office on the other side of Mount Morris Park, that his visit would bring to an end the incidents of which he fortunately had never learned. He walked on one of those splendid New York summer days that last about an hour and was thinking big, generous, humane thoughts. His heart was warm toward his fellow man. That building had developed a weak spot and was unsafe. He might as well tell the tenants to move, since the building had to come down anyway. He wanted to keep a clear conscience.

As he reached the park's sidewalk, he was nearly run down by a speeding car and one wonders what he thought of worrying about other people's troubles.

At that moment Doña Dolores was speaking with bitterness to Vicenta: "I suppose I should be happy enough to sing, after all the misery I have known, after all the misfortune that has piled upon my head. I did not want to say anything the other day about the incident of Angustias's party dress, but the procession . . ."

The usual, unavoidable interruption was advancing loudly along the corridor.

Jerry entered the kitchen and suggested in comically deep tones: "What about food, Mama? I have to rush back for the meet." His voice was changing and his gloom only seemed increased by his puberty.

"It is high time you thought of something else besides playing. If your poor father were alive . . ."

The bell rang. Mr. Goldstein had arrived.

The moment he explained the object of his visit, Doña Dolores put her hands to her head. "Ay Dios mio! Vicenta! Listen to what this man says. The house is going to fall down. This is the very dregs in the cup of bitterness which has been my life. Even the house where I live is going to fall on me, all because poor people cannot afford to live in solid buildings. Oh my God, my God, my

God! When a person is as unfortunate as I am, she has no reason for living. I may as well die right now. Let's get out of here this minute!"

The magnanimous offer of Mr. Goldstein to move to another of his houses was accepted as soon as he had reassured Doña Dolores that all his other buildings were sound, solid as a rock, and the preparations for moving were begun at once.

The next day as Doña Dolores stood on the sidewalk and saw the two moving vans drive away packed with their belongings and heavy furniture, she turned exhausted on Vicenta: "Did we forget anything?" she asked feebly.

"I don't think so, Doña Dolores," the servant answered through a yawn that nearly turned her inside out.

"Well; it would make no difference anyway. We are too poor to own anything of any value . . . . How tired I am!" She addressed her two children who stood there looking very bored and dutifully sad. "All right then, let's go."

The group walked slowly in the direction of the new house.

And the last incident one may accept since one has accepted so many others is that one day after the old unsafe building had been duly demolished and nothing remained but abandoned foundations replete with debris, a tramp was rummaging through and came upon a bundle of dark clothes covered with dirt and dust. He picked it up, shook it and more dust dropped from it, mixing with the other. Having found the clothes acceptable, he walked away still brushing and shaking from them the last traces of dust, without bothering to think whether it was the stuff houses are made of, or the stuff men are made of.

from

Flotsam & Jetsam

Aidan Higgins

In Denmark every day is different; so say the old books. It's made up of islands, every island different, and a witch on each. There are over 300 of them. I knew one of them once. She lived in Copenhagen, that port up there on Kattegat. We were fire and water, like Kafka and Milena, a daring combination only for people who believe in transformations, or like boiling water. You were Mathilda de la Mole.

No, you were you to the end of your days. Why should I complain? The other day I was thinking of you.

The pale Swedish dramatist who lives over on Sortedam Dossering with a distinguished Danish theatrical lady claims that he has learnt Danish in bed. Across the long wall of the Kommune Hospital a solicitous female hand had inscribed a proclamation to the effect that many of the nurses there are lesbian, too. Ten years ago the nurses of this city were regarded as being no better than common whores.

Down there in a basement you had lived like a rat with good old Psycho, in a lice-ridden hole below street level in a kind of cellar, the walls green with mould. Water dripped from above, you suffered, Petrusjka was but a babe. The place was full of furnace fumes by day, rats ran about at night, chewed up your stockings. Drunks fell down into the area. You lived there then. I didn't know you. Where was I?

This Danish capital is a tidy well-run place. The little grey city is relatively free of the subversive aerosol squirt and graffiti-smeared walls of West Berlin; though the pedestrian underpass near Bar Lustig is marked with a daring axiom to the effect that *Kusse er godt for hodet* or cunt is good for the head, with a crude heart pierced by an arrow.

You wrapped newspapers inside your clothes, crouched behind Psycho Kaare, your arms about him, bound for Sweden. That was your life then. All the associations with your lovers seem to have been pre-ordained, moving rapidly towards consummation. He was the third man in your life. Blind in one eye, 192 centimetres tall, a failed dramatist turned carpenter, transvestite, father-to-be of little Petrusjka Kaare.

You lied to the shop-girls. The outsize dresses were not for 'a big mum', but for Psycho, wanting the impossible, garbed in female attire, ill, unshaven, chain-smoking, drinking Luksus beer, looking out the window into the street of whores. There was a strange smell off his breath. Both of you were undernourished, half starving. You left him, lived with an alcoholic pianist for three weeks. Then you couldn't stand it any more—there was an even worse smell off him. Empty turps bottles crowded the WC. You swallowed your pride and approached your mother for a loan. Mrs. Edith Olsen gave it grudgingly. You returned to Psycho, the tall unshaven figure in the chair, dressed as a woman, looking out the window.

Then you were standing for an endless time with your hand on the red Polish kettle that was getting warmer and warmer; knowing that an important moment had arrived for you. You would go to bed with him. He would be the father of your only child. So nothing is ever entirely wasted, nothing ever entirely spent. Something always remains. What? Shall I tell you?

Oh he was a young man once, and very thin. He knew Sweden, had been there before. He arranged the papers for renting a house. It was cheap there then. He was writing one-act plays, a mixture of Dada and Monty Python. They were funny. He sat cross-legged on a chair, typing away, laughing. As a child he had done homework with frozen feet stuck to the cold floor. The Royal Theatre rejected the plays. You loved him. Light came from his face. He was young once; not any more. In his early forties he had begun to grow old. Now he is a dead man.

The motorbike, covered in sacks, hid under snow. All the boards in the hut creaked. Winter pressed down on the roof. In the *dacha*, you and Psycho began starving again. A plump partridge strutted up and down in the garden every evening. Each evening it returned. Armed with a stick Psycho waited behind a tree. You watched from the window. The bird was too clever, Psycho too weak with hunger, the cooking pot stayed empty. You wept.

Then Psycho couldn't stand it any longer and left for Copenhagen, the cellar and the rats. He couldn't take it any longer. You couldn't bear to return and stayed on. You were alone for weeks, made a fire at night, to keep off the living men, and the dead men too. The dead were full of guile and slippery as eels.

Going into Sweden on the back of Psycho's motorbike you had almost died of cold. Motorcyclists are known to experience a sense of detachment, and *may not even recall arriving at their destination.* St. Brendan the Navigator saw Judas chained to an iceberg in the middle of the Atlantic. It happened once a year, by God's mercy, a day's relief for the betrayer from his prison in the everlasting fires of Hell.

But you accepted all the buffetings of fate. You walked into the forest. You said: 'It's difficult to think in a forest. I am thinking *av karse*, but the thought never finds its end, as near the mountains or by the sea. It's heavy in there, the wall of trees keeps out the sun. There is absolute silence in a Swedish forest, no singing birds there. Even the *uuuls* are silent. Oh that was a miss for me.'

In the forest you came face to face with an elk. The great prehistoric head was suddenly there, the mighty span of horns, the mossy tines, set like an ancient plough into the weighty head. You glared, separated by only the breadth of a bedroom. The great beast was grey all over, like a certain type of small Spanish wild flower found in the hills. The dead flower in the jar of the Cómpeta bedroom.

Then, without a sound, without breaking a twig, the elk faded away into the forest. It was very quiet there. Heavy too, like the Swedes themselves. They worked all day, raced home in identical Volvos in the evening, closed their doors. It was a *Shakespearean* forest, you thought, with no dead leaves, no undergrowth, but mossy underfoot. The light there was very dim, angled in, then draining away. *Matterly light*, you thought. Elks moved always in 'matterly light', fading back into the silence out of which they had come. The Swedish-Shakespearean wilderness.

from

Geometric Regional Novel

Gert Jonke

The new law is being posted on all barn walls. Striking hammers drive the nails through the paper made from reeds into the wood. When the points of the nails pierce the paper at the edges, the white fibers rustle. There's a hissing before the nail, hit by the hammer blow, penetrates the barn wood. You can see billposters' hands holding hammers; they position the nails before hitting them, standing on one leg in front of the wooden brown walls, the other leg raised, pulled up, so that the kneecap presses the lower edge of the poster against the wall, as they drive the first nail through one of the two upper corners of the notice into the wood, they then stand on both legs in front of it, pressing one of their arms against the not-yet-fastened upper edge of the paper to make sure that the sheet hangs straight, comparing the border of the top section of the poster with the line of the barn roof's overhang; only then is a second nail driven through the other upper corner; then the billposter takes two steps back so that he can visually assess, with a critical eye, the potential public effect of the announcement on the barn wall; then he steps back up to the wall, takes two more nails out of the pouch lying at his feet and drives them through the two lower corners of the official notice into the barn wood; while he is doing this, you can usually find him in a stooped or half-bowed position, his bottom covered by the billposter's uniform trousers material, swaying back and forth to the rhythm of the blows, to the left and to the right.

Billposters are usually full-bearded people with wire-rimmed glasses, various types of physician's bags, climbing boots, woolen kneesocks, knickers, knapsacks with strapped-on ice axes, felt hats with pheasant, grouse, partridge, or chicken feathers and mountain climber's gear pinned on, who turn up in the remotest parts of the land, are greeted happily by the children because they often give them bent nails, crumpled paper scraps, stretched-out rubber kneebands, discarded rusty hinges in various sizes, torn suspenders, broken-off pieces of barbed wire, and many other things, but have to watch out that the posters they carry rolled up under their arms aren't stolen.

When barn walls aren't available, he nails the announcement on trees, pigsties, benches, farmhouses, grain silos, or chalets; if, in the last case, he happens to disturb a dairymaid, waking her from her sleep if it's early, she awakened by the hammering opens the window right away, waves, and gives a friendly smile.

The New Law:

For reasons of security it will henceforth be prohibited to walk through forests and along tree-lined roads in order to protect the population from the black men who hide so well in the shadows of the trees that sometimes they can hardly be distinguished from the darkness of the tree-lined roads. It is the intention of judicial authorities that the people, who from now on will move o n l y i n the open countryside, can be immediately discovered and categorized by the personnel, geodesists, surveyors, constables, soldiers, and their assistants, who are responsible for their sector of observation; people who come across the h o r i z o n into their sector of observation can quickly be plotted, registered, and classified, two or three times; prior to the time of the new law, despite all deliberate efforts, such thoroughness was never possible, indeed, sometimes not enforceable at all, because the people almost always walked through forests and along tree-lined roads and, for this reason, were, unfortunately, quite often confused with those hiding in the shadows of the trees; but in order to insure that the divisive dissatisfaction this had caused in many segments of the population would be avoided in the future, the new law was passed and ratified as quickly as possible and herewith goes immediately into effect; people who comply will have no further reason for dissatisfaction, those who do not comply, however, will continue to suffer the consequences of breaking the law. Where it is necessary to walk through forests and along tree-lined roads because there is no open countryside yet and the traffic routes have trees beside them, the roads will be precisely designated and specified; personnel will be posted at the beginning and end of each forest lane or tree-lined road and, if the road is very long, at stations along the way; any number of inspections can be undertaken, whose technical and statistical data will serve the republic for the general improvement of the social conditions in the land and, in so doing, are desirable.

Where the forests begin, tables are set up, stakes driven into the meadows, wooden surfaces put on top; whoever wishes to walk through the forest goes to one of the tables, where an official standing behind the table or sitting on a tree stump hands him two forms which are to be filled out and handed over for examination before starting the journey; both forms are then signed, one is stuck in a file, the other is to be taken along and handed over to the other official at the end of the woods. Both forms, differently colored, contain the following, identical questions, which are to be answered truthfully:

NUMBER_____

SERIAL NUMBER_____

DATE_____

TIME_____

NAME_____

DATE OF BIRTH AND PLACE OF BIRTH_____

OCCUPATION_____

PREVIOUS OCCUPATIONS IF APPLICABLE_____

PLACE OF RESIDENCE_____

PREVIOUS PLACES OF RESIDENCE IF APPLICABLE_____

ADDRESS_____

PREVIOUS ADDRESSES IF APPLICABLE_____

WHICH OCCUPATIONS DID YOU PURSUE IN WHICH PLACES OF RESIDENCE_____

NAME, DATE OF BIRTH, PLACE OF BIRTH, OCCUPATION, PREVIOUS OCCUPATIONS IF APPLICABLE, PLACE OF RESIDENCE, PREVIOUS PLACES OF RESIDENCE IF APPLICABLE, ADDRESS, PREVIOUS ADDRESSES IF APPLICABLE OF YOUR FATHER, OF YOUR MOTHER, OF YOUR BROTHER(S) AND SISTER(S), OF YOUR WIFE, OF YOUR CHILDREN, OF YOUR EMPLOYER, OF YOUR FAMILY PHYSICIAN, OF THE EMPLOYER OF YOUR FATHER, OF THE EMPLOYER OF YOUR MOTHER, OF THE EMPLOYER OR EMPLOYERS OF YOUR BROTHER(S) AND SISTER(S), OF THE EMPLOYER OF YOUR WIFE, OF THE EMPLOYER OR EMPLOYERS OF YOUR WORKING CHILDREN IF APPLICABLE, OF YOUR FATHER-IN-LAW, OF YOUR MOTHER-IN-LAW, OF YOUR BROTHERS-IN-LAW, OF YOUR SISTERS-IN-LAW, OF THE BROTHER(S) AND SISTER(S) OF YOUR FATHER, OF THE BROTHER(S) AND SISTER(S) OF YOUR MOTHER, OF THE BROTHER(S) AND SISTER(S) OF YOUR FATHER-IN-LAW, OF THE BROTHER(S) AND SISTER(S) OF YOUR MOTHER-IN-LAW, OF THE CHILDREN OF THE BROTHER(S) AND SISTER(S) OF YOUR FATHER, OF THE CHILDREN OF THE BROTHER(S) AND SISTER(S) OF YOUR MOTHER, OF THE CHILDREN OF YOUR BROTHER(S) AND SISTER(S), OF

THE CHILDREN OF THE BROTHER(S) AND SISTER(S) OF YOUR WIFE, OF THE CHIL-
DREN OF THE BROTHER(S) AND SISTER(S) OF YOUR FATHER-IN-LAW, OF THE CHIL-
DREN OF THE BROTHER(S) AND SISTER(S) OF YOUR MOTHER-IN-LAW, OF YOUR
POSSIBLE SECOND WIFE, OF THE BROTHER(S) AND SISTER(S) OF YOUR POSSIBLE
SECOND WIFE, OF THE CHILDREN OF THE BROTHER(S) AND SISTER(S) OF YOUR
POSSIBLE SECOND WIFE, OF YOUR POSSIBLE SECOND FATHER-IN-LAW, OF YOUR
POSSIBLE SECOND MOTHER-IN-LAW, OF THE BROTHER(S) AND SISTER(S) OF YOUR
POSSIBLE SECOND FATHER-IN-LAW, OF THE BROTHER(S) AND SISTER(S) OF YOUR
POSSIBLE SECOND MOTHER-IN-LAW, OF THE CHILDREN OF THE BROTHER(S) AND
SISTER(S) OF YOUR POSSIBLE SECOND FATHER-IN-LAW, OF THE CHILDREN OF
THE BROTHER(S) AND SISTER(S) OF YOUR POSSIBLE SECOND MOTHER-IN-LAW, OF
YOUR POSSIBLE THIRD AND OF EVERY OTHER POSSIBLE WIFE AND HER IMMEDI-
ATE RELATIVES AND OF ALL EMPLOYERS AND FAMILY PHYSICIANS OF THOSE
NAMED AND THEIR CLOSE RELATIVES AND ACQUAINTANCES AND OF ALL RELA-
TIVES AND ACQUAINTANCES OF THEIR EMPLOYERS AND FAMILY PHYSICIANS
NOT LISTED HERE_____

_____

_____

_____

_____

_____

_____

_____

ARE YOU AND ALL PERSONS LISTED BY YOU SATISFIED WITH YOUR EMPLOYER

(YOUR EMPLOYERS) AND FAMILY PHYSICIAN (FAMILY PHYSICIANS)_____

_____

_____

_____

_____

WHERE ARE YOU GOING_____

WHAT DO YOU WANT THERE_____

WHY DON'T YOU WANT TO GO SOMEWHERE ELSE_____

WHY DON'T YOU STAY HOME IN THE FIRST PLACE_____

WHEN DO YOU EXPECT TO ARRIVE WHERE YOU ARE GOING_____

WHERE WILL YOU STAY THERE_____

WHEN WILL YOU COME BACK_____

WILL YOU COME BACK AT ALL_____

WHY_____

WHY NOT_____

HOW MUCH MONEY DO YOU HAVE WITH YOU_____

HOW MUCH MONEY ARE YOU BRINGING ALONG IN ADDITION TO THAT WHICH YOU

ARE NOT LISTING HERE_____

WHY DON'T YOU WANT TO LIST HERE THE MONEY WHICH YOU ARE BRINGING

ALONG IN ADDITION BUT ARE NOT LISTING HERE_____

FOR WHAT DO YOU NEED THE MONEY THAT YOU HAVE WITH YOU_____

IS IT YOUR INTENTION TO MAKE PURCHASES AT YOUR DESTINATION OR ALONG

THE WAY_____

WHY_____

WHEN_____

WHERE_____

FROM WHOM_____

WHAT DO YOU WANT TO BUY_____

DO YOU ALSO WANT TO BUY ANYTHING ELSE WHICH YOU ARE NOT, HOWEVER,
LISTING HERE_____
WHAT_____
WHY_____
WHEN_____
WHERE_____
FROM WHOM_____
WHY DON'T YOU WANT TO LIST HERE WHAT ELSE YOU ARE BUYING BUT NOT
LISTING HERE_____
WHAT ARE YOUR MONTHLY EARNINGS_____
HOW MUCH DO YOU PAY IN TAXES_____
HAVE YOU EVADED TAXES IN RECENT TIMES_____
WHY_____
WHEN_____
FOR HOW MUCH DID YOU DEFRAUD THE STATE_____
HOW FAST DO YOU WALK_____
DO YOU WANT TO REST ALONG THE WAY_____
WHY_____
WHEN, WHERE, AND HOW OFTEN_____
HOW TALL ARE YOU_____
HOW MUCH DO YOU WEIGH_____
HOW LONG ARE YOUR FEET_____
LENGTH OF YOUR STRIDES_____
DO YOU FAVOR THE INTRODUCTION OF GENERAL TESTING FOR SEXUALLY TRANS-
MITTED DISEASES_____
ARE YOU AWARE THAT YOU ARE A BAD PERSON THROUGH AND THROUGH_____

OR ARE YOU BY ANY CHANCE OF A DIFFERENT OPINION_____
ARE YOU HAPPY IN YOUR OCCUPATION_____
WOULD YOU RATHER TAKE UP ANOTHER OCCUPATION_____
WHICH_____
WHY_____
WOULDN'T YOU LIKE TO BECOME A WOODCUTTER_____
OR WOULD YOU RATHER FIND EMPLOYMENT IN ANOTHER BRANCH OF THE
LUMBER INDUSTRY_____
ARE YOU BY ANY CHANCE SUFFERING FROM VENEREAL DISEASE_____
DO YOU HAVE GONORRHEA, SYPHILIS OR SOFT CHANCRE_____

ARE YOU UNDER TREATMENT_____

DETAILS ABOUT THE INDIVIDUAL WHO STUCK YOU WITH THE VENEREAL

DISEASE_____

ARE YOU UNEMPLOYED_____

WHY_____

DO YOU LIKE FORESTS_____

WHY_____

DO YOU LIKE TREE-LINED ROADS_____

WHY_____

DO YOU LIKE TREES IN GENERAL_____

WHY_____

DO YOU REGARD TREES STANDING ALONE OR IN GROUPS AS ADVANTAGEOUS,

DISADVANTAGEOUS, OR DANGEROUS_____

WHY_____

HAVE YOU ANSWERED ALL QUESTIONS TRUTHFULLY_____

HAVE YOU ANSWERED SOME QUESTIONS FALSELY_____

WHICH_____

WHY_____

WHICH QUESTIONS THAT YOU AREN'T LISTING HERE DID YOU ANSWER

FALSELY_____

WHY_____

WHY DON'T YOU WANT TO LIST HERE THOSE QUESTIONS WHICH YOU ANSWERED

FALSELY BUT AREN'T LISTING HERE THAT YOU ANSWERED THEM FALSELY_____

_____

WHY DON'T YOU WANT TO LIST HERE THOSE QUESTIONS WHICH YOU ANSWERED

FALSELY BUT AREN'T LISTING HERE THAT YOU ANSWERED THEM FALSELY BUT

AREN'T LISTING THAT HERE_____

OTHER_____

FURTHER NOTATIONS_____

NOTATIONS BY THE AUTHORIZED OFFICIAL_____

REMARKS BY THE AUTHORIZED OFFICIAL_____

SIGNATURE OF THE AUTHORIZED OFFICIAL_____

SIGNATURE OF THE AUTHORIZED OFFICIAL_____

SIGNATURE_____

SIGNATURE_____

DATE_____

TIME_____

SERIAL NUMBER_____

Before starting the journey the two forms are to be filled out, handed over to the official for inspection and examination; both are signed by him, he sticks one in a file, the other is to be taken along and handed over to the agent at the end of the forest road.

Individuals who do not fill out the forms truthfully must pay a fine not to exceed the number in today's date in local currency; for illiterates, there are clerks appointed who sit on tree stumps, hold typewriters in their laps, listen to the dictation of the applicants, and fill out the documents.

If you should meet an authorized official in the forest along the way, you have to let him examine the form you brought along, answer his questions genially, truthfully, joyfully, and without excuses.

At the end of the woods the latter form is to be handed over to the agent there.

On the part of the authorities, everything is being done to protect the population from the black men hiding in the shadows of the trees. Despite the new regulation, the population is called upon to be wary, even while traveling on monitored forest roads, because it is suspected that now the black shadows of the trees are disguising themselves in counterfeit or stolen uniforms and molesting, threatening, reviling, abusing, and insulting the people.

Parents and those qualified to teach are urged not to let their children and pupils forget the game WHO IS AFRAID OF THE BLACK MAN in the shadows of the forest.

Prior to the time of the new law, many are said to have disappeared in the forests without a trace. Among executive authorities, where there was no explanation for it, the speculation was offered that the black shadows of the trees and everything that was hidden in them were to blame. However, after the time of the new law many people or even more than before are said to have still disappeared in the forests without a trace. Members of the judiciary offered the speculation that only the shadows of the trees are to blame, which now disguise themselves in counterfeit or stolen uniforms and make fools of the law-abiding population.

But voices were also heard to say that those who disappeared in the forests were actually arrested by the executive authorities because statements taken from their forms indicated that they hide behind trees. People who made such claims are later said to have been reported missing in the forests without a trace or else identified, arrested, locked up as members of the forest's shadows and turned over to the courts by agents.

Who are these black men anyway? Do they live in the shadows of the trees or disguise themselves with the darkness of the forests, or how do they so easily portray the twilight in the tree-lined roads? It is reported by the judiciary that these questions can only be answered when the menace is completely eliminated because only thereafter, based on statistical, criminal, philosophical, psychological, mathematical, economical, historical, biological, physical, zoological, medical, psychotherapeutical, botanical, paleontological, parapsychological, chemical, cybernetical, archaeological, sociological, logical, and many other studies, which, of course, are continually under way, but which can only be evaluated, judged, edited, scrutinized, checked, controlled, and classified after the elimination of the menace, can these questions be answered in a way that everyone will be able to understand. Many, who at first speculated publicly that there were no black men at all but supposed they were only the invention of higher authorities and also a carefully planned pretext under which to justify the new law and its effects and consequences, and much more, because in reality there are only the shadows of the trees, in which no one and nothing can any longer hide, are said to have afterwards disappeared in the forests without a trace or else were identified, arrested, locked up, and turned over to the courts by agents on the basis of their black shadows.

According to higher authorities, there are plans to soon disclose new measures of even greater effectiveness:

the intention is to cut down all forests, tree-lined roads, and, if necessary, fell trees standing alone in the countryside,

because

1. one wishes, once and for all, to rid the population of the threat of the shadows behind the trees as well as those dark elements hiding in them, which then would no longer have any places to hide because there would be no more trees behind which they could hide,

2. should the practical enforcement of the new law become difficult because there are not enough agents available, the aforementioned plan would make enforcing the new law unnecessary,

3. the high rate of unemployment, which exists everywhere in the land and is steadily increasing, thereby would be eliminated by training and hiring all do-nothings as woodcutters or employing them in other branches of wood processing, because the lumber

industry would record a boom like none before, because then much more wood than ever would be available for processing.

The huge supply of wood which will suddenly build up will be utilized to produce,

in advance,

barn floors, barns, bay windows, beams, beaters, beds, benches, boards, bolts, bowls, bridges, buoys, carts, chair backs, chairs, chests, closets, coffins, cots, crates, doors, fences, flutes, footbridges, footstools, forks, gallows, gates, halls, houses, huts, lattices, mats, mills, plates, poles, rafts, rings, roofs, shingles, ships, skiffs, slats, spoons, staircases, stalls, steps, sticks, stools, swings, tables, trunks, walls, wheels,

paper,

anterooms, bedrooms, beer coasters, border crossing gates, bunk beds, chalets, charcoal, customs barriers, dance floors, dining rooms, door frames, door latches, dung pits, floating hotels, gymnasiums, horizontal bars, living rooms, log cabins, matches, piers, playpens, rafters, railroad crossing gates, road barriers, saltshakers, school benches, school compasses, sideboards, slides, table legs, toilet seats, tree supports, wheelbarrows,

artificial limbs, balconies, counting houses, credenzas, figures, hinges, parquets, portals, racks, railings, scaffoldings, trays,

ax handles, baby carriages, birdhouses, book bindings, broomsticks, children's rooms, children's toys, clothes hooks, clothes trees, corridors, doghouses, gangplanks, hinge pegs, hop poles, knife handles, labor camps, nesting boxes, pepper shakers, plank floors, rack wagons, rocking chairs, rocking horses, scarecrows, shovel handles, storerooms, street barriers, window frames, wastepaper baskets, warning signs, traffic signs,

cubbyholes, vestibules,

bar ornaments, bookshelves, butter churns, obstacle courses, paprika shakers, pickax handles, radio tables, toy guns, weekend homes,

granaries, paneling, seats of government,

guillotines,

ceiling structures, inn furnishings, lamp shade frames, screwdriver handles, canal pile planking,

carpentry workshops, telegraph poles,

playground apparatus, riverbank reinforcements,

bay windows in seaports,
bridges for prospective streets,
bay windows for women looking down,
bridges for prospective rivers,
bridges for prospective canals,
scarecrows for prospective nurseries,
bridges for prospective streets across prospective streams, rivers,
canals, waterways, ravines and the railings bordering them, footbridges across prospective ravines for the prospective necessity
of the prospective elimination of the prospective interruption of
prospective mountain pasture paths for prospective foxes, cham-
ois, hares, stags, chickens, dogs, cats, horses, deer, cattle, sheep,
weasels, nanny goats, squirrels, ibexes, skunks, giraffes, camels,
antelopes, dromedaries, elephants, water buffaloes,
and much more;
the wood still leftover will then be stained with tallow or tarred,
kept in storerooms protected from rain, hailstones, snowfall,
humidity, and other harmful weather conditions;
but there are also many who say the whole land will probably
very soon be decorated and paneled with wood.

every step will be a signal knock beneath the grains and knotholes of the wooden boards mounted on top of the ground you will
hear streams rivers and waterfalls rushing between the cracks
of the planks later trodden down the water of the marshes will
rise seep in and the cotton grass will creep upwards

careful planning and the incorporation of cybernetics will guaran-
tee the economic boom in the land,

the marsh marigold will climb up out of knotholes

you see the billposters still traveling through the land, the metal
fittings on their knapsacks glisten in the air, their hammers strike
the barn walls; log cabins are being built in clearings for the agents,
bunk beds for the soldiers; you hear the stakes pushing into the
grass, the orders of the higher officials, the sounds of the typewriters among the shrubs,

blueberry pickers startled herbalists chased away

blackberry gatherers plunge from rock ledges

throughout the forests you hear the chopping of the axes, which
are leaned against the trunks during the noon break; perhaps fall
is coming, yes, that's quite possible,

fall is coming,
one fears chestnuts and other fruits that fall from trees,
to guard against that one holds his hand above his head or wears
a wide-brimmed hat;
snipers in trees and hedges have it harder, they are discovered
more easily.

Translation by Johannes Vazulik

from

The First Book of Grabinoulor

Pierre Albert-Birot

On a shut-in November evening Grabinoulor's feet were sploshing about in the Paris mud and that evening he distressed his shoes no end they were quite astonished at having to plough through such black mud when such white snow was falling for Grabinoulor's shoes are full of logic even when his feet are inside them nevertheless although he was perfectly conscious—which is something that happens even to people who are not in the least conscientious—of how humiliating this state was for his shoes and indirectly for himself too he couldn't do anything that evening other than place his feet on the ground as there was so little space between the earth and the sky and that was why even though he was Grabinoulor it took him a long time to reach the theatre which high-flown declamators were supposed to transport with all its listeners to the environs of the infinite but a gentleman with a nose a mouth round cheeks spectacles ears and a fine mirror-like pate simply by speaking brought the ceiling down on to the head of everybody sitting in the theatre and it was Grabinoulor who was the most inconvenienced by this nevertheless ladies and gentlemen in full possession of their senses—although being in possession of one's senses doesn't always mean that one is sensible—came on ostensibly to make some allegedly poetic revelations but the smart suits of the men-readers remained smart suits and the pretty little dresses of the women-readers remained pretty little dresses during and after just as before and the carved Cupids—for the tenderest representation of love may be carved in the hardest stone—on the stage boxes didn't change places and the colour of the seats remained the same whereas everyone knows that when seats are really deeply affected they change colour and when the audience left it the theatre was still in the same boulevard where white snow that made black mud was still falling which was why they were talking animatedly of the price of butter and the increase in rail fares as for Grabinoulor he opened his umbrella yes really you must imagine as best you can Grabinoulor under an umbrella the fact remains though that they—the umbrella and Grabi—found themselves no one knows either where or when confronted by public opinion whose belief was that the end of the world was nigh not on account of the unfortunate slight planetary impingements predicted for the following Wednesday at five fifteen pm but because of the feminine fashion that was guilty of relying too openly on the beauty of the human body well Grabinoulor realized in time that public opinion is nothing but a hideous toothless old woman that people are in the habit of passing off for an irresistible beauty and he recognized that the world was in perfect and reassuring health since it was virgins who were asked by fashion to reveal the breasts which they have and not grandmothers who only have the remains of them and that was why full of confidence in the future he didn't stay any longer that day than any other day with the old woman with three stumps of teeth and he passed by he walked turned disappeared reappeared and took the train (unless it was the train that took him) now while he was traveling incognito on a suburban line in a bottom class carriage it so happened that at one station a market woman who was truly formidable both because of the fiery colour of her face and the height and width and thickness of her meat got in and settled down comfortably and forever you might have thought in Grabinoulor's compartment opposite a narrow little old woman and Grabinoulor claimed that from that moment on the compartment was completely transformed although he couldn't say precisely what had changed then when the train was just about to move off they saw this mass with its pyrogenic head lean out of the window and shout in a resounding and meridionally-accented voice Adieu trrrrrraou dé kiou[1] then the entire mass came back and flattened itself on the seat or rather flattened the seat laughing a magnificent belly laugh but it quickly became serious and addressing the little old woman said at least you didn't understand what I said just now oh I'm glad you didn't understand it wasn't very polite you know Madame what I said just now but I well you know I'm someone who just can't help making jokes and even though the train had started she leant out of the window again and fired off her joyous cry at the people in the fields 'Oy you lot Adieu trrrrrraou dé kiou' and that day the train took much

1 'trrrrrraou dé kiou' means, literally, 'arsehole'—more or less. Added to the 'Adieu adieu' it forms a popular catch phrase, pronounced in a merry meridional accent, which is not particularly 'vulgar'.

less time getting to Paris even though according to the mechanical assurance of the clocks in the stations it wasn't running any faster so in the evening of that day Grabinoulor found himself cooped up somewhere or other with five or six poets which is as dangerous as watching an experiment in a laboratory of pyrotechnics because the poet is a species of mankind who projects coloured lights of a very beautiful effect when he is on his own but who has the strange characteristic of sending out nothing but asphyxiating or explosive waves the moment he is in the presence of another individual of the same species and when six of them find themselves nose to nose the atmosphere immediately becomes unbreathable or full of sparks which is why it might perhaps be reasonable in order to preserve oneself if not from the explosion at least from the asphyxia to wear a boar's-head mask during these gaseous meetings but Grabinoulor is a being who is both violent and free and who has a horror of anything that restricts and disfigures him and if he reluctantly agrees to hide his flawless body under some costume that is both a great liar and full of sadness exactly as if he were ashamed of this beloved body at least he has so far stubbornly refused to put any sort of mask over his face Adieu adieu trrrrrraou dé kiou which is why that evening he felt some slight seasickness which might also be called salonsickness but when he was back on the friendly asphalt he breathed in the fresh air deep down into his thorax Adieu adieu trrrrrraou dé kiou and even though this joyous refrain produced the sound of a fairground orchestra within the immensity of himself he could still hear the last breath of a fine painter who had just died far too soon after his birth in one of those big houses in the City built especially to go and die in and he could also hear the sound made not so long before by the fragile girl with the long pigtails when her little body with the big child-carrying belly flattened itself on the cobblestones after the death of the painter had precipitated her from a sixth-floor window and these muffled sounds created a silence in Grabinoulor and he aged a notch but he continued on his way because he could still hear the monumental woman shouting out between two hearty laughs Adieu adieu trrrrrrrraou dé kiou

Translation by Barbara Wright

from

Impossible Object

Nicholas Mosley

There was once a Christian governor of Cyprus called Bragadino who was a good and holy man and who surrendered to the Turks on the understanding that he would be given his life and freedom. This was at the time of the Crusades, when men fought with passion and for piety. The Turkish commander was a politician and an epileptic: he promised Bragadino that he could have his life and freedom then cut off his nose and ears and ordered that he should be flayed alive. But all the time he was being flayed Bragadino maintained such a sweet and seraphic expression that several people watching him were converted. And even when his skin was completely off his angelic smile still continued. This gave the Turks the idea of stuffing it and selling it back to his family. His family bought it and put it in a church, as a moral and religious precept.

The crusades were a proper time in which to observe human nature—the pursuit of holiness for the sake of money, the use of torture for the sake of identity, a time of passionate care and commitment. Those who distributed pain were politicians; those who profited, saints. Either way life was not easy; unless you died young, which was recommended.

There was another such incident at this time, performed by women. The crusades were an excuse for men to get away from women, who pushed them out into the cold like seaside landladies. There was a King of Cyprus who went away to war and left behind a wife and a mistress. The former was barren; the latter as usual, pregnant. As soon as the king had gone the wife imprisoned the mistress and hammered her like a mortar with a pestle. This was to produce an abortion, in the pursuit of morality and religion. But the point of the story is that the child flourished; only the mother died. And the father of course too; who was caught with another of his mistresses and castrated.

When babies have their first experience of love they are already as grown men; green things in the hands of older women, lying on their backs and watching themselves being tickled; the endearments like the forearms of executioners. They are called duck, rabbit, turtle; the seagulls come to get them. For every baby born, there are the million or two dead children.

Perhaps the worst torture at this time happened to an Arab who was condemned by a Mongol to eat himself. He was sat down at a table with a napkin round his throat; was served feet first, perhaps; would have had to tell his host how delicious they were, such is Arab hospitality. And there were still the great delicacies. You close your eyes and open your mouth and in nanny pops them. And the eyes. He would not have got as far as the eyes: he would not have been left even with the smile of Bragadino.

The baby crawls across no-man's-land with its limbs shot off by the drug its mother took to keep it happy. It hopes that one day its mother will come to punish it, because then it will know who it is again. It looks out on a world in which slaves walk round with their hands pierced and hung round their necks like identity discs. It is by pain that caring is demonstrated: we were taught this at Sunday School.

So we wait for the aeroplane to come over the mountain, the stars on a clear night so beautiful. Once men found it easy to be hurt; now they have to advertise in shop windows. They ask for someone to order them; to lock them on the wire floors of cages. Sometimes they dream of walking forwards again like mad archaic statues. But first their hair falls out and then their teeth and their spectacles in piles. They have the vision of the sky opening again. This has always happened at the cost of the skin being stuffed; the million or two dead children.

.   .   .

One winter I was doing research work in the reading room of the British Museum and I used to go for lunch each weekday to a public house. This was of the kind where students and young business-men jostle over chicken sandwiches and beer, their arms and talk as impersonal as machinery. This suited me, since I like to feel anonymous in a crowd. I occasionally tried to hear what some of my neighbours said, but I seemed able only to catch laughter or exclamations just before or after words, so that intelligibility was as hard to come by as the pin-pointing of an exact present.

One day there came into this pub a couple, a man and a girl, who stood out from the rest of the customers because of their self-absorption and exposure. The man was tall like something grown out of its shell; he had spectacles and fair hair and was almost middle-aged but not quite, because of some vulnerability about him—a daddy-longlegs. The girl was self-contained and dark-haired and beautiful; she was young but at the same time mythical, like Cleopatra. One or the other would arrive at the pub first; would peer round tables and over screens with the gaze of people intent on hidden music; would go out into the cold or into the rain again to wait because like this they were closer to each other and more comfortable than being distant in warmth. They were in love. They seemed a definition of this term—like dinosaurs of extinction. Love is out of date now because it is annoying to others; exposure causes embarrassment.

A London pub at lunch time has a masculine air; there is an activity of elbows like bow-strings being drawn back at Agincourt, feet are on duckboards and glasses are grenades in the hand. There is a roar of agreement as if in a Paris *salon* that Dreyfus should be shot. I did not like the people in the pub. But I think I am happiest when I feel people are against me.

I was working at the time on a historical book on the relationship between men and women. What interested me was man's view of woman as either goddess or mother or prostitute; and woman's acceptance of these roles for the sake of her identity. I was studying in particular Christian attitudes at the time of the Crusades, and contrasting these with attitudes in classical Greece and Rome.

When the man and girl came into the pub—they would have met out of doors and come in holding on to one another—there were not only the ordinary manifestations of love, the clasped hands, smiles, the gazing on one another like hypnotists; but a further dimension as if they were actors trying to make reality more real than it might be. They seemed to want to prove that love was real by demonstration—an existentialist proposition. And yet they were oblivious of the people around. I had remarked in my work how romantic love seemed to have withered as a result of self-consciousness: the couple seemed not to be unaware of this, but to avoid it. It was as if they were constructing, or honouring, something called love which was separate from themselves; as if they were artists.

The girl had a small dark face surrounded by a fur hat from which her gold eyes looked out. I thought of Anna Karenina at the railway station; her first appearance there and the last, because her end was foreshadowed in the beginning. In the girl's eyes was a depth like a well; you could drop a stone down and listen for ever. When she walked she strode with long legs as if she were skating. When she took her hat off you expected snow to scatter.

The man was older than she. He wore a black overcoat and a brown muffler and seemed always to be looking for somewhere to put his gloves. He did not take his coat off; he wrapped it round him as if he also were waiting for a train. But I could not think so romantically of the man. I was jealous.

The couple ignored the other people in the pub, who ignored them. There was something narcissistic in their rituals: they held hands too long like opera singers, had to keep time to their hidden music, were dragged forward and back and lost momentum. There is an instance in *The Valkyrie* when Wotan and Brünnhilde have to step towards each other across a stage and to keep pace with a drawn-out climax; their movements are absurd, but also beautiful. The couple were like this.

I usually had a book propped on my knee for something to do between eating. I used the book as a shield, just lifting the pages and shaking crumbs off.

I had noticed the couple for several days before I watched them closely. I think I became interested then partly because of my work. I had had the idea that men wanted to see women as goddesses or prostitutes because these are men's own projections and they have to find objects to accept them or else their own nature becomes unbearable. I remembered a fairy story by Oscar Wilde in which Narcissus looks into his pool and asks the water what it thinks of him; and the water answers that it sees its own reflection in his eyes.

I did not at first hear much of what the couple said. They did not speak much. When they met there were a few of the murmured nonsenses of love; I heard him once say that she looked beautiful and she answered, as if it were a poem—Oh so do you! She had a voice which sometimes bubbled like a fountain. Then they would sit and hold hands underneath a table; rock backwards and forwards as if playing chess. Eventually time would be running out and they would have to order food. I think that they half fostered their absorption so that they could remember time suddenly and feel tragic; he could get up and go to the bar with the Furies after him, and she could watch him disappearing from a distant shore. At the bar he would widen his eyes and gaze at the top row of bottles; live in memory of the table he had just left. Then he would return, and the girl would greet him as if they had been apart for years. They lived in a myth, which was real to them.

I began to build up some imagination about their lives. The girl wore a wedding ring. She sometimes carried gramophone records. I thought she might be a music student. She would play the harp or flute.

The man might be a second-rate conductor. He would fall off his rostrum, flailing at windmills.

At any rate they were both working in the vicinity and were using this pub to meet in at lunch. I did not know why they had nowhere better to meet. The girl was married; probably the man was too. They were not married to each other. I thought—Perhaps all love has to expose itself, since it exists in memory and expectation.

One day when the pub was more crowded than usual and there were no more free tables they had to come over to one at which I sat. This closeness was unnerving; I was suddenly faced with my imagination, like acquaintances meeting in a nudist camp. The girl in close-up was even more beautiful than I had thought; she was in her twenties, probably a mother. Her skin had that quality of the self-possessed; there were no rivers under her eyes for her to cry down. The man had a clown's bright gentleness; he waited for the tea-tray to fall about his head.

I held my book on my knee. It was a book about the Etruscans. The Etruscans were one of the few people of the ancient world who had treated women with dignity. On their tombs husbands and wives lay in each other's arms. This could not have happened with the Greeks and Romans, who were homosexual.

I did not really want to hear the couple talk. The impression that I had of them was that of a silent film. I liked the self-absorption and fluttering of eyes and the long pauses; the impression of white horses rushing across deserts. Speech, self-consciousness, had killed love. You could not lie on a grassy bank and spout Shakespeare.

The man was saying "You cook for him. Clean. Does he expect you to have feelings?"

He had a drawling, upper-class voice, slightly fading at the edges.

Just before this, when they had come in, he had touched her cheek with such triumph.

He said "Anyone can have feelings. On a Saturday night, with you-know-what and a bath."

The girl shook her head. She was eating a chicken sandwich. He waited for her, but she did not speak. I thought she at least might preserve her poetry. When she looked at the man her eyes had the ability to go liquid.

He said "What are you thinking?"

They did not seem aware of myself. They spoke to one side of me.

The girl said "I'm totally destructive."

The man shouted with laughter.

He said "Of course. The difference between you and others, is you know it."

She shook her head.

When they leaned towards each other they were like blind people putting print into a machine: they could not know what would come out of it.

She said "How are things with you?"

He said "We're in different rooms now."

She raised one eyebrow.

He dropped some food on his lap and swore.

She said "How are the children?"

He said "They've got a new girl friend. In pink tights."

Her eyes were pearls cutting down through her eyelids.

He said "How is yours?"

She said "Oh, she climbs all over me."

I do not remember much more of this first conversation.

I had been interested in them because I was lonely: I cared about love. One sees so little of it. Also I had this theory that only in a mixture of cynicism and romanticism was love possible. But I had not expected it in others. I did not know now if I liked it. I wondered how much from myself I projected on to them. Such processes are in the unconscious.

The couple did not come to the pub again for some time. This was around Christmas; I thought that they must have gone to their separate homes. I missed them. I was living so much on my own that this friendship of phantoms was important to me. I did not have a girl friend at the time. I loved women; but because I could not easily have myths about them I think they sometimes feared me. And perhaps I was afraid of them, that they might destroy me.

Then one day the couple were in the pub again before I had arrived. I was so pleased to see them I almost acted as if I knew them; greeted them like one of the characters in their story. I had already begun to think of them as characters in a story—both the one that they seemed to listen to like hidden music and the one that I was even then thinking of writing. They gave this impression of something being constructed by artifice; which they watched unfolding passively, yet also created. I believed that all life was like this; and they were people uniquely who recognised it. I recognised it myself, and so was involved in their story. But perhaps we could never let each other know; like spies in a foreign country.

But I thought I would be brave and sit at their table.

They were in one of their silences in which love existed like a charge between thunder-clouds. I was still half cynical: I thought that people who acted love so openly must underneath be devouring. When I sat at their table the man looked at me and for a moment I thought he might recognise me; but he recognised nothing. The girl, as always, was sensual. She had taken her coat off. There is a girl in a Moravia story who is very young but when she takes her clothes off has the voluptuousness of an older woman. This girl was like that. The two of them were under some strain. They seemed to hover slightly above their seats like hummingbirds. I thought they might be meeting for the last time. I put my beer down quietly. The man was doing his rocking-chair act; a Cezanne in the evening. The girl's lower eyelids had gone slightly up as if heat had contracted them.

The man was saying "If we went off with each other we'd break within a year. There's a love that destroys you, which is what you've got, and that frees you, which is what you haven't. If you want love then you have to be both together and apart. This works. The other doesn't."

She said "You don't really want me."

He said "I do." Then—"You'll see one day."

They were not eating. Their food remained on their plates like the helpings which come back to children at lunch and tea and supper.

She said "I want us to have some sort of life together. I think love is a common world which you build from day to day. If you don't have that, you don't have anything."

He said "We've got everything."

She said "We've got nothing."

He looked exhausted. He had wrapped his coat around him as if in cold. His mouth was stiff and his words were difficult to enunciate. He said "All poets have always known, that you can't have love by grabbing it. You've read the books. For God's sake."

She said "I'm not a poet."

He said "You are."

She looked like Judith going to Holofernes.

He said "Once society did it for us. Now we have to do it ourselves."

She said "What?"

He said "Make impossibilities."

She said "What's the point?"

He said "To maintain ecstasy."

He spoke like someone making a confession under torture.

She said "All right keep your beautiful marriage."

He did not seem to hear this. He put his head back and closed his eyes.

He said "One does build from day to day. But one adds, one doesn't destroy."

She said "You risk nothing. Nothing'll break you."

He said "Or one loses the lot."

They were silent for a time. They seemed refugees preferring to die than look over the hill to the promised land.

He said "Why don't you leave him then?"

She said "Because you don't want me to."

He said "I do."

She said "I think I have a great capacity for love. I could give myself totally."

He said "You do it then."

She said "I can't bear deceit."

She spoke in her operatic voice.

He said "All life is some bearing of deceit. That's human nature."

She said "I don't believe that."

He said "Ducky, I know you don't."

She said "What?"

He began to tremble.

He said "Like Anna Karenina in the railway station. You spread a little happiness around."

She stood up. She said "That is unforgivable."

I wanted to say—I thought of Anna Karenina!

He said "Oh sit down."

She opened a bag and took out a pair of keys and put them on the table.

The keys lay there like things untouchable except by pincers. I thought—So he did have somewhere to take her. He paid no attention to the keys. I thought—But she won't be able to go now. She went to the door. I thought—He'll go after her. He did not even look up. She went out. The keys remained; one with a shaft like a gun barrel.

I wondered for a moment if I might follow and see where she lived: then I might make a date with her.

The man finished his sandwich. I wanted to say to him—Just because it is impossible, doesn't mean you stop trying!

After a time he stood up. He was the exhausted soldier after five minutes' rest on the march, strapping his pack on and setting out for the firing line. I thought he might still go after her. But he went to the bar and ordered another beer. And when he came back I saw that he was smiling. His was one of those faces that you turn upside down and it comes out different; the clown becomes the cossack. I wondered how he did this. He sat beside me again. His face had become gentle: a cunning child's.

I thought of my story about this man and the girl who looked at themselves in mirrors, who moved the opposite ways from what they intended. I might make the man be living like myself alone up four flights of stairs: the girl coming to make love mornings and evenings. They would use their lunches purely for public purposes; needing an audience because observers influence that which is observed. Or perhaps they did not make love at all, being so concerned with their maintenance of ecstasy.

After this there was another gap of a week or so in which neither of them came to the pub. I felt as if I had missed my opportunity to speak. The man of course had picked up the keys and had put them in his pocket.

Then one day the girl came in on her own, stepping as usual

with long legs as if on ice, peering serene and purposeful and still with no rivulets beneath her eyes. I sometimes think this look of hers was simply because she was short sighted. There was nothing unusual about her coming in alone; the man would follow. I waited with my book propped up. I was reading Suetonius. In Suetonius, men and women do little except murder one another. I suppose at first sight I am not very noticeable, being short, shorter than the man—though I look quite like him. The girl gazed across at me and I thought she might recognise me; but she did not; she went to the bar and ordered her sandwich and fruit juice. But she did not go to wait in the cold. And after a time the man still had not followed. I wondered whether they had arranged their usual rendezvous or whether she had come in just by chance. After a quarrel they would both be proud; they would not telephone to make it up. They would prefer to wander in the streets on the chance of casual meetings. I thought I was getting to know them now. In a casual meeting there would be no resentment nor triumph: they would hope for miracles. But still the man did not come. Her face began to look as if it were being hit. I tried to imagine her with her husband and child or children. She would go out each day to study music. Her husband would be a thickset man with well-cut hair. They would sleep in a bed with a canopy like a sea-shell. She had finished her sandwich and still the man had not come. I wanted to talk to her. She was standing picking the petals off daisies to see if she existed.

I thought I could ask her to have lunch: tell her all about the conductors of hidden music.

She waited three-quarters of an hour and then went out. She had looked at the door often. I had not spoken to her. I think she was too sad. Grief is private, because so exposed.

Then the next day the man came in alone. He was so un-self-conscious that you could feel his wondering about himself; looking round tables, over partitions, and asking what he was doing there; making the observations that other people would make if they had been interested. He pulled off his gloves and scraped them down his sides. I thought perhaps he was one of those artists who would burn his life's work because he did not have enough wood for a fire; and this would be convenient for him, because his work was not good enough. The girl did not come in. I did not think she would. I thought that their luck had run out now: or perhaps they were purposely missing each other for the sake of their guilt and ecstasy. He ordered his beer; tapped on the counter. I wondered if he knew what was happening. I thought—He is being forced to be responsible. I have these theories. His sad face flashed like a lighthouse. I wanted to say—She was here yesterday; you should ring her up. But I did not. He did not ask me; he did not ask anyone. I thought—We all have our self-destruction; mine is that I don't tell him. He was so noble he would go to the scaffold smiling. He waited, and then went out.

And then I regretted bitterly not speaking to him, because it was on some trust in my doing this that both he and I depended. If we were working for love, I thought, then it was just some chance as this that might effect it. I was a stranger: love is a matter not of arrangement but of grace: I could have said—She was here yesterday—and then he would have telephoned her. Love is impossible for people in it but not for the stranger; there is the ghost on the street corner, the face in the dream, the accident by the church yard. The happy outcome of love depends on the chance good-will of others. I knew this. All the other people in the pub were working their arms and mouths like oil-drills. Within love is the curse of opposites; you cannot force them, you can only let them grow. But the stranger can break in and impregnate them like a sperm. I had not done this. I had been jealous of him.

I wished to God I had taken hold of him on the bridge of a ship in the gale and had said—Angels do sit on the masthead!

After this there was a spell of cold weather in which the pavements froze and all the young men came into the pub happy because their legs had nearly broken and they had just missed being run over by buses.

Then the man and girl came in together again one day having met just outside; they reeled through the door as if into a bedroom. I thought they were really going too far this time; their hands were groping over each other's backs, sides, coat-tails. I thought—They are too old for this: God sits behind a two-way mirror. Their smiles had gone into skulls with pleasure: they were climbing up each other as if on a rock-face. I wanted to say—Go out into the street again; you can do it better in private. I did not like them then; they were making me feel deformed. The pub was too crowded to sit down. The man was saying over and over again "Oh I do love you!" and the girl was saying "Oh so do I!" I was standing by them in order to get more beer. The young men had their tankards up like boxing gloves. The man and the girl were still clinging to each other. There is a moment in making love which is like the end of a four-minute mile: I wanted to jostle them and shout—Keep going! She was saying "I don't know how you can ever forgive me." He was saying "I never have anything to forgive you." She said "You are so marvellous!" He said "So are you." I wanted to shout—Come on, ref, break it up! I had to push my way between shoulders. I said "Excuse me. Thank you."

He was saying "That had to happen. Didn't you know? You have a genius for love. If you hadn't hurt me, where would we have been? Or if I hadn't hurt you. You're too good. I know you can't bear deceit. It's I who am wrong. I'm trying to change. You're forcing me. It's your instinct, which is true, and my knowledge, which knows this. But look, it can't be easy. We're trying to do wrong, and doing right, and this is impossible. But we can. How do you break things? There's something happening. But we have to go at it backwards. There's one racket, power, and another, love. But love is total; it leaves nothing out. It runs you. What do you think life's like? I'm not going to say any more. You can't expect miracles. You trust. Don't you?"

She said "I trust you, absolutely."

They went to a table and sat stupefied. Every now and then he opened his mouth and then shook his head. Their hands were under the table like elephants grasping buns. There seemed to be a curved drop of concrete in front of them.

After a time she said "How are the children?"

He said "All right."

I do not remember this time how they left; whether they or I went first, whether I watched them out of the door still reeling like wounded soldiers. I remember his giving her back the keys. I think I saw them still at their table as if in some final tableau; the curtain going down and up concealing and revealing them; the crowd standing and moving for the exit. The life of characters in a play is only in their performance: in the empty auditorium are ghosts.

There was another long gap. It became so long that I thought they must finally have settled to go to their room instead of eating chicken sandwiches. Or they might have quarrelled again. I thought—I know the rules; he was wanting to have his cake and eat it; but you don't go on for ever getting more loaves and fishes.

In the spring the atmosphere of the pub changed from a Turkish bath of elbows and overcoats to the bright stillness of a linen cupboard; the doors suddenly opening on to cherry-blossomed streets and cars bright like axes. I had quite given up hoping to see them again. I sometimes dreamed of them because I did not know the end of their story. I wanted to write of them coming across each other again in the distant future. And then one day the girl did come in once more, alone. She was without her coat and fur hat and was dressed in jeans and a striped cotton jersey. She had had her hair cut. She looked like a boy. For the first time in the pub all the men noticed her. She had the sensuality of opposites—the youth and experience, the leanness and voluptuousness, which invited both protection and sadism. Her hair was in a fashionable style shorter at the back than at the sides: you could pull it like bells. There was a large label on the seat of her jeans. She was looking round the pub and not really expecting to find anyone. She was there for the memory. I think I knew then that I loved her: that I could now speak to her. It was not that I had really been afraid before, but simply the power of imagination. I stood. There was a feeling in my throat as if I had put my hand between her legs. Then I saw a man who had come in behind and was staring at her. She had her back to him. This was a man I had not seen before. He was elegant with dark curly hair. I knew that he was to do with her. She had not noticed him. He seemed to be waiting for her, or driving her, as if she were a pony: or as if he were a footman behind a queen. So I could not speak to her. I wanted to tell her that he was there. I knew her situation so well. Then she turned. She recognised him slowly with her short-sighted eyes. She did not move her feet; she swivelled her body, so that her back was still half to him. I thought—She is having it both ways. There were diagonal creases along her jersey and jeans. She said "You!" He smiled. He was different from the other man: he would not need to bang his head against walls to come out smiling. She had opened her mouth and pearls were cutting down her eyelids again. He said, copying her—"You!" He had a voice like a madrigal. Her face began to change—first into the look of being hit which I had once seen when she had been with the man (her man; I felt as if I were standing in for him; this other man was obviously her husband) but then into something hawklike, almost predatory; her top lip lengthening into that of a Red Indian. The husband wore a grey suit and white tie; he looked as if he were picking up a sailor. He said "You didn't expect me." Then—"Do you meet him here?" I thought that her man—the original man—might be about to come in: I could go out into the street and warn him. Then I could at last step into their drama. But I stayed where I was. She said "Did you follow me?" She stood with her head slightly back as if the smoke was in her face with which she sent out signals. She said "Do you have people following me?" She did not sing now; her voice had a slight accent; as if from a flat land with wheat fields. He went on smiling. He jingled money in his pocket. He repeated "Do you meet him here?" She waited; a chieftainess with her eyes on the hills. Then she said "No." He said "Do you promise?" She said "Yes." I thought—She cannot bear deceit. They looked at each other. They neither of them believed.

I found myself getting up and going out with half despair, half anxiety. I felt something bruise about what I had felt about love: I also wanted to see if the man was coming. I had been so happy to see her; I myself was in love; I was in the street on a bright spring day looking out for someone to meet me. I thought—We can no longer be shocked; we find ourselves on corners, beneath windows, and we do not know how we got there. But we would rather be there than anywhere else. I might lay down my cloak in some puddle—for her or for her lover. I might think I was waiting for my own girl with dark hair. But I was not. Ultimately we make no contact; not with anyone, not with ourselves. I was in the street for a breath of air. I turned back to the pub. My beer and sandwich were on a table. The girl and her husband were at my table. I said "Excuse me." She still did not recognise me. She was after all short sighted.

She had such a beautiful skin with a glow coming from the inside as in Venetian paintings. Her husband said "Why do you come here then?" The blackness of her hair made her mouth red and her eyes gold; colours were built up in layers by time and by tradition. He said "You never go to pubs." His watch-chain was gold: he was rich: perhaps the other man was poor. The husband said "Well?" I wanted to say—Tell him you meet a girl friend. She said nothing. She crossed her legs and pulled in the small of her back. In this position she showed off her body.

He said "I know you meet him. You were hoping to meet him today. Why do you lie? You were once honest. He won't come back. He won't do anything for you. How can you love someone who doesn't love you?"

She said "I wasn't going to meet him."

He said "I love you. I'd do anything." He took hold of her wrists.

I thought—Crash the tables, knock over the beer mugs.

He said "You are so beautiful."

A look of peace had come over her face. She stared down at his fingers as if they were bracelets from a lover. I thought—She is in love with pain; she will get it from him.

He said "Come and have lunch."

She said "I've had lunch."

He said "Here?"

He looked round the room with its clanking of human machinery. He seemed amazed. Then he noticed me. He was the only one of them who ever did notice me; as if it were his duty to distinguish natives.

She began to pick his fingers off her wrist. They were burrs from a hedgerow. He had leaned half across her lap. She placed his hand on his knee. He said "Do you love him?" She said "Yes." I began to pick up my books. I thought—They are well suited. There was the look on her face of an eagle above fur. His was a neck with the crowds going over him; he would live full of medals and of glory. I did not want to stay for the end. You know when it is the end because of the change in the music. Everyone gets up and leaves the cinema. She and her husband would lead a good life, the seashell above their bed and the dinners for six people. You avoid the National Anthem and find yourself in the street. It had been raining. You copy the people in the film; take a deep breath and go off to the sunrise.

I tried to analyse, after I had gone, what it was that had happened. I do not know about marriage—I have not been married myself—but it seems to me that what men want from women is a mixture between doll and mother so that they can push the doll around and make her pretty and then, when she cries, ask the mother to punish them. Which she does. This is perhaps the best a woman can do for a man—to be pleased at his weakness. But it is impossible. What a woman wants from a man is a mixture of god and victim—then he can be pitied—but she only tolerates someone who is cruel. This is safe. But neither a god nor a victim is cruel.

I returned to my own life; my own impossibilities. My work at the British Museum came to an end. I made plans to go on a trip to Rome, which is another story.

It was on one of my last days at the pub that I saw the man come in again—her original man, the musical conductor. He had brought a woman. I knew the woman was his wife: he had not even bothered to get her to follow him. She wore dark glasses. She had a face of delicate and strong melancholia, the good contours slightly gone, as if from rain. Her dark glasses were worn to hide something underneath; not from the sun, but the rivulets people cry down. The man was holding her by the arm. She did not look round the pub, did not seem interested in it. He took her to the bar. I saw that she might still be beautiful; was tall and drawn as a film star. He asked her what she would drink. She looked round the bottles and said she would like water. She must be his wife, to ask for water. He leaned right over the bar to make this special request for her. He drummed with his fingers. I remembered all these mannerisms of his: I thought—He will suddenly look round the room and remember he has been here before. Perhaps he even wanted his wife to ask him—Have you been here before?—so he could pretend to be amazed, and say—Yes. She had short brown hair; she drank the water as if it were precious to her. The man looked round: at the oak fireplace, the hunting prints, the elbows like machinery. Perhaps he had remembered he had been here with a girl. His wife suddenly asked him "Did you meet her here?" He said immediately "Yes." I could hear this quite clearly. I had come to the bar to order beer: I had no illusions that he would recognise me. He still gazed round. Perhaps he heard the birds singing. He said to his wife "You knew then?" He put a hand out and patted her behind. She remained motionless. Then she made a face as if there was something bitter on her tongue. He said "Oh that was a long time ago." He chanted this. The woman drank. He said "Do you want me to talk about it?" She did not answer. He hummed. I suppose he often had to have these conversations with himself, having no one else to talk to. He looked towards the door. This was where they had come in, had clung as if under a waterfall, had climbed up each other's rock-face. His wife said "Why did you bring me here?" He said "To exorcise it, ducky." He said this very quickly. Then he said "Don't you want me to exorcise it?" I wondered if she ever answered. He drank some beer. I thought—He will always enjoy his beer. His wife said "Do what you like." Then she smiled. I thought—These people surely cannot last; they will be overwhelmed by what they are doing.

.   .   .

I did manage to forget about the couple then. They lived on at some level of mind because they were still symbols of what I believed about love—of its complexity, even of the necessity of this—but they became unreal to me as people. I thought that they had possessed for a moment some secret about love; but they had betrayed this.

I finished my book on the relationship between men and women: I went to Rome; travelled through Italy. When in Turin I wrote the story about the man and the girl at their future meeting. But this became mixed with a story about myself, and had to be fitted into a larger context. I remembered how I had had the impression that I was a character involved in their story as well as they in mine; and none of us yet knew the endings.

Then some time later when I was travelling in Morocco—a year or so, I do not know; we become confused about age; we do not want to remember it—I saw the man again. I did not at first recognise him: I was not sure where I had seen him before. I thought he might be a colleague from a previous metamorphosis; an academic, perhaps, or a fellow-officer in the war. He was wearing shorts and a dark blue shirt and was holding a beach ball. He was pouring with sweat. He was standing in front of the plate-glass window of a hotel. This hotel had been put up by the government to attract tourists; it was on stilts over the beach, an edifice like a whale. In the plate-glass my vision was doubled; as if the man were standing both inside and outside himself. I was not staying in the hotel; I was in the Arab part of the town, in a room above a cafe. I still did not quite believe, after I had recognised him, that he could be the man in the pub: you see someone in unexpected surroundings and you have no way of fitting him in. The face is no help; everyone has a face; you have to wait for something mutual. He has to be as uncertain as you, in order to create accustomed surroundings. The man had a large rather muscular body on thin legs: Englishmen abroad seem to stand like birds. The plate-glass window reflected the beach; the wind blew sand against it, the lines of waves came in in tiers, they made a trough where the man was standing. I was at some distance, staring at him. His face was redder and more aquiline. I tried to reconstruct what I remembered; his figure a windmill amongst overcoats and elbows. There were three children in a group beyond him waiting as he held the ball; they were boys, bronzed and indolent. I remembered that he had said he had had children—or that might have been in the story I had written. There is something primitive in a group of boys by the sea; they wait to be engaged in some contest with horses and fighting. Beyond them was a young child, a girl, playing alone in the sand. She had dark curly hair and was tiny. I knew it was the man and yet I could not prove it; if I spoke he would not know me, and he might not want to remember the pub. Yet there is always the chance of talking to strangers in a foreign country, and I had despised myself for never having spoken to him before. I thought I could just go up to him and say—I sat next to you one winter; you won't remember me. It was extraordinary how much he sweated. I went up to him and said "You won't remember me. I used to see you in a pub." People make a show of recognition; raise a hand and let it hang above your shoulder. He said "Yes I remember." He had that drawl. I was touched. I thought he might say—Fancy seeing you here! He held out his hand. I took it. I thought—He is confusing me. I said "Do you really remember?" He said "No!" He laughed. I remembered his way of enjoying embarrassment. I said "It was a pub called—" I mentioned its name. I did not want him to get away with it, but he looked delighted. He shouted "Oh!" as if the sky had reopened for him. He said "Then you must meet—" He turned and waved his hand towards the hotel. I thought he was suggesting that I must meet his wife. I remembered I had never really liked him. He said "What are you doing here?" I said "I'm writing a book." He said "Oh you write too?" When he was interested it was still as if it were only in himself. I said "I once wrote a story about you." He said "About the pub?" I said "No, about a journey up through Italy." I thought this at least would interest him. He said "I wrote a story about the pub."

He was looking towards the three boys. He did not want to introduce me. He began again. "You must—" but he often did not finish his sentences. He looked at the hotel. I thought I should say—It's all right, I won't tell your wife about the girl in the pub—but then I remembered his wife knew already. I thought—He expects people to drop off trees for him. He said "Do you know this coast?" I said "No." He said "I was at Tamanet after the earthquake." I said

"I know." He said "How?" I said "I mean, I know there was an earthquake." He shouted with laughter. I thought—People must sometimes land on him like apples. He said "I meant, I once wrote a story about that too: you might have read it." I said "What was your story about the pub?" He said "It was told by a man who had seen us that winter." He banged his head. He said "But you can't exist! Or you're myself. You see how this is impossible!"

The three boys on the beach were waiting for him to play with them. They resented the intrusion of the stranger. I could not place the small girl with curly hair: there was no other family on the beach, and she did not seem to belong to them. The boys were pushing at the sand with their toes and picking it up and hopping on one foot. I waited for his wife to come out; she would be wearing dark glasses and would trust the sun like a lamp she knew would not burn her. He said "Don't go!" I had not intended to go. I wanted to involve myself at last in their story. He threw the ball to the boys where it landed in a pool and splashed them. The small child suddenly put down her bucket—she had been building sandcastles—and ran towards us. She moved with her legs kicking sideways as children do by the sea. She ran right past: I thought she must be running to her mother. I saw that the girl had come out from the hotel. I had not expected this. It was as if she, too, were reflected in my memory double. She was walking towards us and she seemed to have nothing on. There was the way she walked as if on ice, her long legs bending very little at the knee, her boy's and woman's body, the black hair that made her colours so remarkable. She appeared to be seen from two directions at once—both full-face and in profile. The Egyptians had painted like this; with the legs and head sideways and the body straight to the front. You can only get the whole of a person by this sort of art, deception. We all seemed to have been waiting for her. She wore a two-piece bathing suit spotted like a leopard. The boys by the sea seemed holding the reins of horses. The small child had jumped up into her arms. The child was her daughter. The spaces between us were confused; there was a light separating and connecting us. I thought—There are people in the unconscious who stand like this: I am frightened of something so powerful and empty. She seemed to absorb all the light around and turn it to gold. The man said to me "Do you remember—" He mentioned her name. She stretched out her hand. The boys in the background had not moved: I thought—they might have been done some great injury; the sons of a tribal king with no wives left. I told her my name. The man said "He used to sit next to us in the pub that winter." The girl said "Yes I remember!" Her whole face lit up. I burned with it. I said "Do you?" Her voice had bubbled over. The child in her arms was struggling to get free: the man took it: it pressed itself in front of his face like a screen. She said "You used to be reading books in Latin." I said "Yes, how clever of you!" I knew I was still in love. I wanted to ask—How did you get here then? I had not expected them to manage it. I had always known that they had possessed some secret. They had not betrayed it.

One of the boys was coming over to us. He was the eldest, tall with dark hair brushed forwards like feathers. He went up to the woman and said "Are you going to bathe now?" He said this gravely, as if he were her tutor. I noticed again how her face seemed exposed; something peeled, translucent. She looked at the man and waited for him to speak: he was tickling the child. The child was fighting; was trying to embrace him. I wanted to tell them how happy I was to find them; that they had proved something that I had hoped but not believed about love. I wanted us all to stay on this beach for ever. I said "How long have you been here?" The man said "About a month." The girl turned to the boy and said "All right, I'll come." This was in her operatic voice; a decision to embark on a long journey. I could not bear that she should go. She turned to me and said "Are you staying?" I said "In the town." I got the impression then that she was asking me to rescue her. I did not understand this. The boy waited. She moved towards the group; their backs to the sea and the reins on their horses. There is an image of a queen being lifted on the shoulders of acolytes, before she is placed on the pyre. They reached the edge of the sea and stood there. I thought—Perhaps she cannot swim. The waves beyond were taller than she; like the steps of a building in an earthquake. She walked into the water and turned her back and fell into a wave. The boys moved cautiously round her. Then she began to swim. She swam expertly. The man was still holding the child; the child was snapping at him. The man pulled his head back. I thought—They should not be doing this in public: then—All this has happened before. I wanted to ask him how he had managed to achieve love; what he thought would happen later. The others were swimming out to sea; her arms and feet like moonlight. I thought I might offer to hold the child for him; I am good with children. Then he could join the others. But he put the child on his back and called out "Hold on tight!" The child stopped struggling. It put its arms round his neck and clung there. The man waited for a moment and said to me "What was your story?" I said "About the future. A meeting." He said "Good." The child was strangling him: he put his tongue out. He seemed so often to be acting. He said "We'll be seeing you then." He ran down to the sea with the child on his back kicking as if he were a pony. The waves were much too high for them, the heads of the others were far out like oil. I wanted to shout—It's too rough! But I thought that they would always be people who would run into danger, because of their secrets about love and what was possible.

from

Billy and Girl

Deborah Levy

Why did the chicken cross the road? Because its mom disappeared and its dad set fire to himself. What that skunk Billy doesn't understand is that pain is not a riddle. It's a mystery because we lack crucial information. Billy's skin is blue. In all weathers. Indoors and outdoors. Blue like the soil on Jupiter probably is. If they ever put Billy into a spaceship and spin him up to the planets, I know he'll feel at home so long as he can take the TV and a stash of popcorn with him. I bought him a cowboy shirt to keep him warm. It's got pearl buttons and an extra one sewn inside the cuff in case. Billy always checks the emergency button is still there when he puts it on. It comforts him just about more than anything else. He wants an emergency button for everything: to get out of nightmares, to call for help when the lift gets stuck, to get out of boring conversations.

Got a tattoo inked into his scrawny upper arm. An old-fashioned one like some virgin boy sailor who called men 'sir' and choked over his first Lucky Strike in a foreign bar full of hookers. I mean, I can't believe he had that dopey tattoo done like all the other fat blokes in the world. It's an anchor entwined with roses and doves. It says Mother, of course.

I don't know why my mother called me Girl.

Sometimes I think she was just too lazy or too depressed to bother calling me by my proper name, Louise. So there are two of me: one is named, the other unnamed. Louise is a secret. No one knows about the Louise part of me. Girl stuck and that's how it's always been. Louise is England's invisible citizen and when I read statistics about how many people live in this country, I always add one more: Louise.

When I was seven, instead of learning the times tables off by heart I learnt the name of every single cleaning product. My mother didn't want a daughter, she wanted a slave girl. Instead of running through parks in little black patent shiny shoes and green ribbons on the end of my plaits like girls do in storybooks, I ran about the house in my knickers with a dustpan and brush. My hands were always in bowls of dirty water washing plates or tying knots in black bin liners full of rubbish. The day I sat my art O level at school all the other kids brought in bowls of fruit and vases of flowers to sketch in charcoal for the still-life exam. I brought in a J Cloth and an aerosol of furniture cleaner and signed my drawing 'Girl'.

Billy never had to lift a finger. Not only was my brother given a name, but my mother used to dab lavender behind his ears even though he looked like a cocky little evangelist from the day they tore him out of her body at the hospital. Listen, I am no slave girl. I want to be a love diva.

Thing is, no one has ever taught me how to kiss.

Louise is waiting for her prince. He will find her, and gallop towards her on a horse. Every single horse in England must be counted so that Louise will recognise the steed when it comes towards her; she will point and say, 'Of course I knew it was going to be that one, the fine white stallion I saw in Kent from the car window.' They spoke silently to each other through the glass of the window and Louise knew she had chosen him and he was destined to find her. Girl says, 'You really make me puke lizards, Louise. I'm going to cut your long hair with nail scissors. I'm going to cut the horse into steaks and eat it raw. I'm going to carve DANGER into your arm with glass. Listen: the spirit of the Horse and Prince have got into the hollow tubes of your nervous system. It's a conspiracy. It's a bacillus like tuberculosis, wheeze and cough it out of your body now!' But Louise doesn't listen. She's waiting for the big day. The prince is Dad.

Dad topped himself. He was a lorry driver and used to show me the big teddy bear he'd hung up in the cabin for good luck. After he died we had to throw away his clothes. The sleeves of his favourite Elvis-style shirt spread out like Christ on the cross. A hero. A saviour. A king. I've forgotten how he died. Oh God. Bring my father back to me, safe and sound. Give him back his face. Give him a salary so he can do a weekly shop. Let him buy me a snooker table for Christmas. Give him spirit (hope) so I might catch some of it.

Give him electricity (light) so I might see him. Give him words so he might speak to me in my hour of need. Give him another chance so that he can spread honey on my white-bread sandwiches. Give him back with a brand-new skin cleansed of pain, but mostly give him back with a wad of tenners in his back pocket, because that will make him happiest and he can drink a pint without fear in his heart. A poor man is wrapped in pain.

After Dad got burnt, my mother took Billy to visit Grand-Dad in Newcastle. 'He's got a glare in his eye, your boy,' the old clown wheezed when he caught Billy's stare and found himself trembling. My mother just stroked his forehead like she always did, mad about her boy. She cried over his bruises. Dad said he'd never hit his son again. But it was like Billy encouraged him. Even when he was a baby he was doing pain research. Crazy for Billy. When Mom disappeared, Grand-Dad was supposed to come and look after us. He did for a while. And then, all of twelve years old, I told him to go. We couldn't stand his jokes. Ever been to Ducksworth? How much are you worth? It was more than I could bear. Knock knock. Who's there? You. You who? Yoooohoooo! A month of that sort of grief I suggested he go home, which is what he secretly wanted to do—and just send us money instead. We did not want our young minds damaged by Grand-Dad humour. 'What's the point of having shampoo when you can have real poo?' It's a good thing Grand-Dad left sharpish. Better to have his cash every week and draw him little pictures on thank-you paper.

I love my brother. He is a crippled angel, flying and falling seven days a week. This boy is a genetic engineer because ever since our mother disappeared, he invents a new mom to love him every night. Read his beautiful lips. Ready steady go!

Yeah. Horrible, isn't it?

Billy smells of Colgate and chips. Sometimes he burns a cork and draws a little moustache on his upper lip. This is his manliness. I mean, who is he supposed to have learnt how to be a man from? Not Dad, that's for sure. But Billy, who might never become a man, only a play man, a parody of a man, is going to win me and him a new world. A world without pain. Is that possible? Christ, sometimes I wish I had rheumatoid arthritis and a sweet young nurse would explain it was a chronic degenerative condition and send me to physiotherapy twice a week. Pain is the suburb of knowledge we grew up in. Little houses crowded together, narrow streets and dodgy lampposts. Pain has unanchored us, sent us raging down the nerve pathway to Patel's English and Continental Groceries for chocolate bars.

.   .   .

Billy and Girl thought they were heading for California. Knew all about America from the brochures and TV. Imagined themselves drinking daiquiris under the palm trees and blue movie skies. 'Cept it wasn't the big buck agents, the surf and Disney pets that wanted them. No Mickey and his lovely first lady Minnie in her lickle white gloves to welcome Billy and Girl to the land of plentiful. No TexMex was to pass their lips. No tax-free shopping in Tijuana. No healthy walks through miles of mall to stretch the legs and get blood circulating pronto to the remaining shards of Billy and Girl heart-hacked with English weather problems. No Florida crocs and beauty-queen mermaids to tickle their pain history and stretch lips into knowing kitsch smiles. Girl was never to become a Nevada cowgirl sprayed into denim and photographed for gentlemen's leisure mags. She thought she would be wearing high-cut orange bathers and shooshing her peroxide flurry hair when she spoke to male lifeguards all muscle and morality and mega-hormone narratives. Poor Girl. I mean, can you see her scrawny white-bread English thighs lazing with the Californian beach girls? English Girl with her introspection and minicab rage and no cosmetic surgery to armour her and no sweet talk inside her to simper its way out and get involved with local boyfriend and beach-life issues? Girl buying donuts in bulk to bait every obese woman she meets into giving her an interview? Hi, Mom. Have a donut. Have three. No. That's all over.

.   .   .

Billy was not to be discovered by Hollywood highballs on Malibu beach in his Speedo minitrunks. Not that kind of boy icon. For a start, even with a tan, even with a personal trainer in a deluxe Malibu gym, Billy is not reliable or predictable. He can't be trusted to learn his lines. Writer delivers script. Director reckons this is the one to swipe all the Oscars on the big night and he is already getting his wife to write his speech. She's faxing a draft to him right now. How he discovered William The English singing 'Twinkle, twinkle little star' whilst strumming a toy plastic banjo, and how he just knew, with Great Director's Instinct, that the boy was a screen God for the contemporary world. Billy is wined and dined, groomed and flattered. Billy eats with gusto. Bloody steaks flap off the sides of his plate. Fistfuls of Californian french fries are shovelled into his boy mouth. Billy never has to eat another chicken winglet again. He gets a little plumper but won't do arm curls, not even with the starter weights that even a poodle can lift effortlessly with one manicured pawkin. He reads the script. Agrees to be a star. He'll play a sulky James Dean reincarnation called Jonnie. His co-star is an apple-pie babe with attitude and her character is called Candy. They go over the script together and then the big day arrives. Billy has to be dragged kicking and screaming out of his trailer and pushed onto the set. The scene is set in a moody bar.

JONNIE: See you're drinking beer.
CANDY: Yeah. So what?
JONNIE: That's a good brand.
CANDY: I know.
JONNIE: Mind if I sit here?
Candy shrugs. Jonnie sits.
JONNIE: I feel really good sitting next to you.
CANDY: (*Secretly flattered*) Well, thank you.

Not too demanding, is it, Billy? Lights. Sound. Action.

BILLY: See you're drinking beer?
CANDY: Yeah, so what?
BILLY: That's a good brand.
CANDY: I know.
BILLY: Mind if I sit here?
Candy shrugs. Billy sits.
BILLY: You remind me of my sister.
CANDY: (*Improvising for camera*) Oh.
BILLY: She won't let me fall in love with other girls.
CANDY: Is that right?

BILLY: I don't mind. Cos I'm frigid.

CANDY: (*Catching director's eye. He's saying busk it.*) Uh-huh.

BILLY: Completely totally fucking frigid.

CANDY: (*Cracking up now*) We'll do something about that, Jonnie.

BILLY: Frigid.

DIRECTOR: *Cut cut cut cut!*

Okay. The English boy has a kind of anti-charisma that's interesting. Inneresting. Let him ad lib. Look at him. He's taking out a little pen knife and cleaning his fingernails. That's not in the script either. Okay. *Okay.* But hang on. Frigid? *Frigid???* Can't have boy icon say he's fuckin' frigid. Not good for box office. Not good for the plot. Not good for the next scene when he has to take Candy home and make love to her in the shower. Cos the only power Jonnie's got in this movie is his bad-boy sex appeal. So why not give Billy England a chance and try shooting that shower scene? See how that goes and then come back to the bar. Okay. So Candy's in the shower, Jonnie's got to take off his kit, climb in with her and soap her breasts, real slow and sexy. Thing is, Billy The English won't take off his clothes. No matter director and art director saying he can keep his pants on. This boy doesn't even wear short sleeves. No way. Says in England he showers in his anorak. That's why it's waterproof. Director thinks, Let's get a little experimental. Why not? We're ahead of schedule. Let him.

Lights. Sound. Action.

Billy English fully clothed gets into the shower with naked Candy. He takes the soap. What does he do? Starts washing his fucking hair. Standing under shower in anorak washing his hair. Inneresting. Only thing is he's got lines scripted for him by the writer who is sobbing into his script, shouting something about never working again. Never let the writer near the shoot. Big mistake. Jonnie is supposed to say, 'I've been wanting to do this ever since I first saw you in the bar.' Do what? Wash his hair while naked nubile looks on? I mean, what kind of pervy movie is this?

So now actress playing Candy is going berserk. Wants to call her agent. Says why don't she wear her skis in the shower? Hell, why not eat a Caesar salad in the shower? Director gets an idea. He's not giving up on Billy England. Says to Candy, 'Okay, sweetheart, tell you what. Talk dirty to Jonnie while he soaps his hair in his anorak.'

Okay. Camera's rolling. Candy narrows her eyes. Voice honey low. 'Hey, Jonnie. I want you to do things to me.' She presses her breasts against his anorak. What does Billy do? Billy screams. Got soap in his eyes, hasn't he?

Director turns to camera. Genuine disbelief. Gestures to Billy. Someone take him away. Hang him. Mince him into mad Heritage British beef patties and feed him to the welfare single mothers and their bastard brats.

Billy informs director that he's got a pricking pain all over his nerve fibres. He's not quite sure where the site of his injury is but he's researching the whole phenomenon and it's his life's work. All he knows is that pain is a black box full of mystery and one day he will unpack it for the reading public. The boy feels he has to explain further. The whole crew gather round. Make-up, continuity, gaffers, all-purpose electricians, the extras playing pool in the makeshift bar, the runners and boom-swinger guy who seems to be in some sort of shock because his arm is frozen in midair and he's muttering something about an aeroplane overhead when he's not even record-ing. Every time his eyes graze those of Billy The English, he shuts them tight so he doesn't have to put a face to the whining voice cracking into his head, wasting his time, encouraging the director to go berserk and sack the whole crew while he recasts.

Billy is saying, See, it's a chronic interdependent kind of pain, a union of what the Greeks call the psyche (mind) and soma (body). He, Billy England, is perfectly aware that he is addicted to his pain. It is his narcotic, and he must give it up and endure cold turkey etc., but before he can do this he will have to find a way of declaring his grief before he can reshape it. Finally, Billy gasps breathlessly, finding an opportune moment to reach for a smoked-salmon bagel from the catering staff, is the director familiar with Freud's description of cancer of the jaw being like a 'small island of pain in a sea of indifference'? No? Well, he, Billy, is the small island of English pain in the Hollywood Hills, could someone pass him another bagel pleeeese? No, not salad. No, not egg mayonnaise. Billy England is a neurosurgeon of the mind—he will build stone cities, carve into rocks, build railroads of the mind, but for now his own soul-tissue damage precludes the possibility of being a boy star.

When the director's jaw actually drops open, culled into silence by this gobbling goofy goy guy ranting in his wet anorak, Billy can see the thousands of dollars of dental work that have been put into the famous director's teeth and gums. Billy wants that kind of attention too. Not in the dental department, though. No. Billy is not reliable. Girl knows this. Look how he nearly sawed through his wrist to create a small diversion in FreezerWorld? Billy. Gulp.

Billy and Girl are Mom-and-Dad pain bonkers. FreezerWorld lucre. They counted their stolen loot again. Minicabs came and went through the night. Girl has some distant memory of being Empress of Minicab Empire. But the infrastructure had gone. Bombed itself into oblivion. Call another cab. She punched in the numbers, dazed and shivering. Practising her big smile. Wiping it off again. Arranging words in some kind of order, not knowing what they meant. Bad-tempered drivers banged on the door and left cursing without a fare. Eventually the minicab office banned all calls from number 24 Harkham Road. Billy and Girl can't even drag themselves to bed, never mind into an aeroplane full of potential Mom-check material.

Counting the notes, skipping numbers to avoid the catastrophe of counting in sequence. Girl saying, 'It's a respectable cash haul, Billy.' Big smile on. Big smile off. 'It's a respectable cash haul, Billy.' On. Off. Billy waving his bandaged arm, whining. Wanting haddock. Moaning for haddock. *Haddock?* What the fuck is haddock? It's a fish, isn't it? Is it? Nothing is certain any more. California? You grind it with glass, don't you? Chat shows? That's one of seventeen words for snow, isn't it? The doorbell ringing. Another aborted cab. Counting the money over and over.

Six hundred pounds.

.   .   .

Not exactly a mega robbery. Not exactly. If they're lucky, it's two cheap fares from a bucket shop. Plane diverted via nine destinations, having to endure the company of cheery sunseekers spilling airline boeuf stroganoff over their hideous T-shirts. Girl dressed in her Jackie Onassis outfit. Shades and a little red suit with white trimming. No tights, just her silver loafers. Complaining bitterly to the stewardesses about the lack of cocktail know-how. Doing her nut when she asks for a Bloody Mary and the air hostess hands her a miniature Smirnoff and a can of tomato juice. Screaming for real service. Demanding half a teaspoonful of horseradish, Tabasco sauce and a lime wedge in her fucking Bloody Mary. Billy howling, biting the cushions when she changes her mind and insists on a Bosom Caresser. Five parts brandy, two parts Madeira, etc. Girl might look like Jackie and Billy does his best to act presidential, but they're not exactly set up for idle luxury once they arrive in California, are they? Only Grand-Dad's envelope of cash, and that's not predictable if he hasn't had much luck on the horses. No. Unless they luck out and get spotted immediately? Like at the airport, showing their visas to immigration. A Pain Agent behind them. Her big blond hair gleaming with the latest monkey-gland sheen spray. Yards of fingernails painted orange. Tapping them against her perfect teeth. Sussing them out. Converting their English pain potential into US dollars. Pain Agent's best catch yet! Whispering into her mobile. 'Al, I jus' hauled in the biggest tuna the Golden State's ever clapped eyes on. Buy a new freezer, I'm draggin 'em home.' Not exactly.

Six hundred miserable English pounds.

FreezerWorld let them down. The Basket People let them down. Louise let them down. The Express till to nowhere. A robbery to nowhere.

.　　.　　.

The morning after, Girl cleaned the skirting boards and Billy swept the kitchen floor. Billy scrunched up newspaper, soaked it in meths and scrubbed every window in the house. Girl washed down the sofa, armchair and curtains. Billy collected every odd sock he ever owned and rinsed them in biological. Girl took all her bras out of the drawer and soaked them in bleach. Billy undid his bandage and gawped at his stitches. Girl trimmed her fringe and then burnt the blond ends in an ashtray. Neither of them answered the telephone. The answermachine whirled and clicked and the voice droned on and on. Always the same voice. Girl rubbed suntan oil into her cheeks and lay on the carpet reading a thriller. Billy sliced one mushroom for ninety minutes. Girl washed the suntan oil off her cheeks. Billy put his bandage back on. Six hours and four messages later, Girl pressed the Play button. Yes. Definitely the same voice on all the messages. Girl searched for Pause, and then she called Billy. As soon as he saw his sister's face he knew he shouldn't have rushed slicing that mushroom. Sat himself down on the most comfy armchair, crossed his legs, fiddled with the laces on his red trainers, asked his sister whether she wanted to rub more suntan oil into her face before she pressed Play? No, but she has just spotted a speck of dust on the woodwork and would he mind if she takes a moment to dampen a J Cloth and remove it? Of course not. And while she's in the kitchen looking for the J Cloths, would she be so kind as to put a lid on the dish with the sliced mushroom inside it? With pleasure. In fact, she'll clean out the fridge while she's there to make room for the dish with the mushroom in it. Perhaps while she's doing that, Billy could take the gold bands off the butts in the ashtray and save them to make a Christmas card with? What a good idea. Why doesn't he make a little box to save the gold bands in?

Girl presses Play. The same message, four times. Dad's voice in their front room. Speaking to them. Dad leaving a message for his kiddies.

from

Mordechai Schamz

Marc Cholodenko

Mordechai Schamz went to the swimming pool last summer. Upon sighting those practically naked bodies by the waters, he took to thinking—no, it wasn't actually a thought, but rather a feeling, a sensation, more precisely. The sensation took hold of him that this spectacle was not for him. What is a spectacle? he said to himself, what is this something that is given us to see if not an offering, a present, a promise, yes, the possibility of a possession? Concerning this possession, its manner, no doubt, could never be made precise to our mind, and yet this imprecision subtracts nothing from the subtle reality our feeling confers upon it. Perhaps because the possibility is what counts more than the possession. And from what is possible, obviously, nothing can be subtracted. And this question of possibility is precisely what I refuse. Or rather I see it refused myself, by myself—that is more exact. Even so I would need to know what this possibility is. How could I find this out? What to choose, within this spectacle, that could become the object of an eventual possession? Must I, in the end, choose: is not the totality what is offered me? No doubt: here is the water, here the bodies, their nakedness, but also what is concealed from me, the faces, the beautiful blue sky, the boards, the bathing huts (oh oh—the huts), and from the unified whole, myself not being allowed to disregard or to distinguish any feature, something manifests itself to my mind, which my mind refuses to recognize and does not want to admit. Is it a single word? Several words of a single sentence? An entire sentence? A speech? Or something else entirely? What is the point, however, of this interrogation since I refuse to answer? All that I will know and all that I want to know is that from this refusal I draw the day's happiness. Yes, here is a day most calm and most cheerful. A most lovely day. And, breaking off there, Mordechai Schamz went bathing.

Such a gaze he has, this Mordechai Schamz! Such a gaze! He's a sorcerer. He deserves neither praise nor blame: as you know, this is the way it is with all sorcerers. The instant his gaze falls upon you, you find yourself clothed in loose-fitting, solemn but nonetheless plain garments. You sense that, if you were to make the slightest move, the clothes would behave exactly like water at night in this atmosphere steeped in secrecy, and create brief shimmers of light. You alone are important in the heart of a new world where you are held by Mordechai Schamz's gaze. Nevertheless, the impression has faded, and now you could not really explain what was so peculiar about those eyes. The man himself, as a matter of fact, does not strike you as special in any way. What he has that's exceptional he holds fast around himself, like a swarm of very tiny birds that otherwise might risk escaping. This must explain the gaze: he lowered his guard for a very brief instant and let it escape. He is a man like any other; you were simply distracted for a moment and, what's more, his eyes are not even large. There's nothing about him that sets him apart from the hundreds of people you objectively see every day. As for the subjective experience, perhaps he leaves behind, briefly, the regret of not having taken him by the shoulders so you could tender your eyes once again to his gaze and assure yourself that it really didn't happen. This experience of being present face to face with him in a place other than where you found yourself. But, as for the feelings a man inspires, each one of us can say everything, and even invent everything, with no risk of incurring any sanction from reality since in such a matter objectivity cannot be said to exist.

Quite recently, Mordechai Schamz bore witness to an accident—more precisely to its immediate aftermath. In all likelihood, it had only just occurred when he passed in the vicinity of the scene. He did not stop. Who does not have, at these moments, the idea of putting himself in the victim's place, simultaneously with a thought of gratitude for the providence that has spared us, yet once again, such a fate? Thus it was, of course, for Mordechai Schamz. Then, persevering in this direction, he wondered what would become of him if he found himself in the place of the person he had just come across. But no answer could be hoped for. It was but possible to vaguely dream of such an eventuality. All told, he continued, such is the way we live each passing moment—and the process is so habitual that a bit of blood is needed at the very least to make it remarkable for us. Our world consists only of glances we have of its periphery, with no hope of ever seeing anything but what we are able to imagine. It is empty, and consists only of our dream of what the surrounding worlds are. Absent to itself, it is composed exclusively of the equal absence of the worlds it verges on. Quite like a road: a road exists only by virtue of the space it displaces, traverses, and continues through unawares. Whether it go on, madly seeking to pierce its neighboring secrets by every conceivable detour, turn, and zigzag, it would not to any less a degree continue to be the very thing that pierces and traverses in ignorance. In conclusion, he concludes, one hardly is, and the little that one is, consists of what one is not. Thus Mordechai Schamz went on, continuing along his path, for he could not do otherwise, all the while saying to himself that what he had so hastily thought (this is the only way he can think—with the idea that his thought is something real, existing as an object, and whose nature is to flee him) had perhaps been distorted by the very haste which had conceived it.

A memory from the early childhood of Mordechai Schamz. Do you remember the poodle Dagobert, Mordechai? A large, very elegant beast, always impeccably groomed, lion-style. What have you learned since you knew that expression? Anyway: it is winter-time—autumn's final days; a pond bordered with trees at dusk, under a sky that had been uniformly leaden all day long; he no longer knows how far from the water, leading he doesn't know quite where, a stairway, very wide and very short, a single flight but whose steps, long and low as they are, seem to the little man as so many landings. He had climbed a few when the incident took place, in connection with the dog. He never found out if this connection was one of causality or simultaneity. This he knows, and he remembers in the language of his boyhood: there is the dog and he falls. His parents told him that he had fainted. As for him, he only remembers the tumble on the stairs, before the water, under the sky, with the dog. He even recalls the smell of the dog, unless it be the scene's itself. Therein are found the numberless components of the incident, all compressed in the memory of this smell, and which he will never be able to separate from each other, isolate in words, sentences, thoughts. It's a great loss, for the incident had its importance, and its importance was held in its components, and its components are now found in a place that is not within his intellectual power to attain, ignorant as he is of the space comprising it. A loss, no doubt, but of what? Mordechai Schamz says to himself. It is in this way, in the end, that all things remain with us that were important: through memory, emptied of what they were, of the fact they were important.

While Mordechai Schamz was walking along in the street, this sentence came to his mind: When my heart opens, it's like a stone splitting apart. It surprised him, since he could not attach it to any of his preceding thoughts and, especially, because it was based on nothing. Had he ever actually felt his heart open? Well, no—even less so this stone splitting apart. Yet it seemed to have imposed itself upon him as an obvious fact, the pure truth. *The pure truth*—a striking expression: perhaps, after all, the truth must never have been in contact with experience for it to reach us utterly pure, and present itself intact to our eyes. The more he sought to discover in his past an experience that might render it objective and the more this search appeared vain, the more, in an opposite way, was strengthened within him the feeling of the obvious fact inspired by this affirmation that seemed to have been made by itself. In the end, why not accept it as an element of information provided by an authority, of which he had not the least proof that it might not be as infallible, or even more so, than that of his own consciousness? Thus he did, and polished the formulation in the following manner: When the heart of Mordechai Schamz opens, it is like a stone splitting apart; this stone having grown hard not only through all the pain undergone by those which it made to suffer but furthermore by all the pain it has spared itself (if one grants that a heart which has already suffered its share, by opening, must leave place equally large for all the happiness it can conceive, to all the pain that others have borne in its place), then, once estimated the exceptional density of the matter needed to be dissociated, an idea can be formed of the force necessary to open Mordechai Schamz's heart. Despite everything, he had no clear idea of what that meant—along with the feeling of having somewhat exaggerated.

Observant and sensitive as he is, Mordechai Schamz was born to be a poet. But if the Muse, until now, has not offered herself to him, it is because he has never opened his arms to her. About her, nevertheless, as about the effects her company had upon others, he knows far more than those who fancy themselves in her favor. Obviously, not the slightest envy nor contempt; that's not Mordechai Schamz's style—and then, is he not far more the poet than they, a poet of life? It is a statement of fact for whomever has seen him, if only for a brief instant. Everything in his look and his ways proclaims it: Mordechai Schamz is a bird and what to a bird are the branches of trees, the state of the air and the prodigality of the fields, such to him is life itself. The matter requires an explanation, and yet how to provide it? Is Mordechai Schamz a bird because, like a bird's, his gaze never seems to settle or because he seems not to have any attachments or because he seems not to have any feelings or because he seems always on the point of leaving? To affirm one or the other of these things would be only to explain appearance by means of appearance, one comparison by another. But what an explanation cannot provide, perhaps an example will. Thinking one day about poetry and about what held him back from composing some, Mordechai Schamz said to himself: would it not be a good thing to live only on charity! To expect everything from someone other than oneself! Not only for drink, for food, and for lodging but equally for sight, touch, smell, thought, sleep, dream and even giving! And this thought for a long while placed him in a great state of exaltation. Of course these thoughts, this state, ephemeral as they were, could equally well be considered as appearances; but what we know of the bird is also appearance.

Translation by Dominic Di Bernardi

from

Night

Vedrana Rudan

I'm looking at the Ikea clock on top of the TV. The television is on, but the sound is off. There are some old women talking about something or other. Or maybe they aren't old. They just have grey hair. And no teeth. I'd look like an old woman too, but every three weeks I pay Alexandra a hundred marks to dye my hair red. I've spent four thousand marks on dental work so I can laugh with my mouth open. But . . . I don't laugh like that. When I was fourteen, the dentist pulled out my top left incisor. For years I laughed with my mouth closed. We were poor. My mother, my grandmother, and I. I bought myself my left tooth for my twenty-fourth birthday. I didn't have a big smile even then. I still grin that way. I'm lying on the bed in Kiki's pyjamas. Striped. Benetton. And, you ask, what does the upper tooth have to do with pyjamas? What is the connection between pyjamas and a tooth? This constant explaining is exhausting! Trying to connect things. Finding the subject, predicate and object. Why should anything in my life have any connection with anything else? Why are you so obsessed with connections? Logic. Causes. Consequences. I'm telling you: I'm lying in bed, I'm wearing Kiki's pyjamas, I'm looking at the clock. What time is it? What's that got to do with anything? And under the clock is the television with a picture but no sound. None of this has any connection with anything. I'm giving you the facts. Your questions piss me off. And your impatience. And that you need to look for drama in my lying here. Something happened. Or is going to happen. Something must happen. Because neither of us has nerves of granite or any other stone. You're human beings who can put up with a lot, yes, but even your patience has a limit. So if I just go on lying and talking nonsense, if nothing happens, you'll tell me to go fuck myself. You're full of shit. What do you expect of me? I'm not Shakespeare or a popular writer. I'm Tonka. I'm simply lying in bed. And staring at the clock. Kiki's in Ljubljana. OK. Maybe there's some drama going on. I've decided, when this night fades . . . What a good word 'fades'! Good one. Good one! When this night ends, I'll leave my Kiki. Leave him. Lock the door behind me. Open a new chapter. Burn all my bridges. Screw the past. Kiki can go to hell. Walk out into a new morning. You're relieved. I can hear you. You're saying, Great, here's some drama after all. It's not just about a stupid bitch lying in bed in the middle of the night—it's not the middle of the night at all—alone and awake for no reason. Something's bothering her. Come on! Let's hear it! What's up with you, you old cow? How do we know you're old? You have a sickly, trembling voice . . . We hear the shaking. Come on! Faster! Kiki drinks? Cheats on you? Doesn't fuck you anymore? Hits you? Why are you going? Are you crazy? Now? You're old! Think about it! You've got a husband, for God's sake! Hang on to him! Wait! Hold on! You're leaving? At your age? You're *not* fucking leaving! So why did the man of your life go away? What's he doing in Ljubljana while you lie around in his pyjamas? Why don't you like me? Why are you such cynical jerks? You're not interested in my story. Why are unhappy stories the only good ones? What do you want from me? Why are you hurrying me? I can't shove my whole life into three sentences just because you're in a hurry. What's the hurry? What's round the corner? Whose insane life are you going to look at next when you get yourselves out of my bed? Here. It's time for a little chocolate. Of course it drives me crazy that I can't live without my chocolate. Fucking candy bars. OK. I'm not going to go on about chocolate. It's distracting you. But it's important! Important? What's important? I'm leaving my husband and going off with my lover who is—a fact that will be important to you—twelve years younger than me. Tomorrow morning, at seven, when you'll be in your offices, stores, or beds because you're unemployed, or at the Job Center, or dying, or fucking some slut, or under your wife, or on top of your fat husband, or next to your skinny little lover, or in front of your fat-headed boss, an Italian, or German, or Austrian, or Hungarian, or . . . I'll be opening the door of my home to my young lover . . . What a word *home*! I'll have my little Samsonite bag in my hand, I won't give a fuck about all the little things that show you have a life, wedding photographs and my daughter Aki's first tooth. I'll throw myself into his arms and grab him by the balls with my left hand. Our neighbor Tomi will see me. He always sees everything, the old shit. He'll think I'm a slut standing there in the doorway of my own home. But he won't know, the old shit, that I'll only be a slut for a short time, a very short time. And then I'll become the owner of a

new man. Officially. We'll get married. Yes. I'll have to get a divorce.
So will he. Miki. Why a divorce? Why all the talking? And why is
my lover called Miki, when my husband is Kiki? You think I'm
playing with you? That I'm confusing you on purpose? That, while
I'm talking, I'm giving you a chance to mix up 'Miki' and 'Kiki'?
Actually, I'm letting you know there's not much difference between
Kiki and Miki. I'm trying to tell you that all men are the same
. . . You're real pricks! Why are you so obsessed with messages?
I'm trying to tell you something? I want to confuse you? Do you
ever think at all? Has it ever occurred to you that no one wants to
send you any kind of message? Or tell you anything? Or tell you
the truth? That someone wants to fuck you up? Manipulate you.
Exploit you. Not communicate. OK. That's communication too.
You're right. 'I want to fuck you up.' That's a message. But I don't
want to fuck you up again and again, not even once. Kiki's called
Kiki, and Miki Miki. Why? What a stupid, stupid question! I don't
want to answer such a stupid, meaningless question. Why am I
called Tonka? Get it? What a stupid question! In fact I shouldn't
give a damn about what you think of me. But I do. I want to tell
you my story somehow, but I wouldn't want you to see me as a
menopausal idiot in her fifties . . . *There*, you see. I'm past fifty, but
. . . OK. I would like you to hear my story, but not to think that it's
all because of the war. I used to be different. And then the war
came and I went nuts. Lots of people went nuts, including me.
PTSD. Post-Traumatic Stress Disorder. Come on. To get a 'post'
trauma, you first have to have the trauma. Come on. I'll tell you
my story. And you can think what you like, but if my story is a
trauma, yours is too. I've thought a lot about this. What's the point
of leaving Kiki? What's Kiki done to me? Why couldn't I forgive
him? What couldn't I overlook? But does someone have to batter
me, gouge my eye out with a fork, put out cigarettes in my cunt for
me to leave him? Why couldn't I leave Kiki because he's good?
Familiar. A book I already read. A village that wasn't destroyed.
A river that flows murkily by. A bell on a bell tower that never goes
wrong. Ivo Robíc and you're just seventeen. Why? Have you ever,
you women who stay married, spent Sunday evening ironing while
he was on the couch playing with the remote? You've got a back-
ache, the children are outside, the electric bill's not paid, nor is the
rent. He's fat or thin. Familiar. At first you're glad because the pile
of un-ironed clothes is getting smaller. And then you stop. And with

the iron in the air . . . Wait a minute! I'm forty! Or fifty! Or thirty, fuck it! I'll iron this pile, sit down and rest my back. And then shove the dishes into the dishwasher, take a shower and lie down beside this *thing*. I've lost interest. But this is my fate for the coming ten or twenty or thirty years. Has it ever occurred to you, you who stay with your husband, to press the hot iron into his face and, as he screams, to lock the door from the outside and go away? Forever! No? That's never occurred to you? You're lying, lying, lying bitches! What lying bitches! Who am I talking to? Who are you? All right. OK. Why are you lying? Do you think you'll be in any less of a coma if you lie? If you've fooled yourself, you've fooled the whole world? As though the world cares about your problems! The world doesn't give a fuck about your pile of un-ironed clothes and the moron you're going to spend the rest of your life with! But this, this thing you're living . . . This is life? And I'm a slut, am I? I'm a slut because tomorrow morning, at exactly seven o'clock, I'll be taking Miki by the balls and leaving? That's why I'm a slut while you're saints? Have you ever waited for your five-year-old child to say: 'I won't.' Mommy's Darling. That's what you call the thing. And you nearly sent his head flying across the room with a slap. Blood gushed out of his nose. And that calmed you down. Really calmed you. Because that was that. Whenever your mother phones you and starts talking in that little quiet voice like someone dying in a burning desert . . . Don't tell me, don't lie to me that you don't want to strangle her with your own hands. Why are you constantly figuring out how much a sick father costs you and how much you'd save if . . . Nurse, pads, medicine, treating his bedsores . . . Come on, you fucking liars!

Translation by Celia Hawkesworth

from

Out of Focus

Alf MacLochlainn

I knew that I had been asleep though not for long enough. The eye-sockets had the seared feeling of having been rebored for insertion of red-hot threaded bolts; the carapace of the head burned with the tightness of a metal helmet shrunken on like the rim of a wooden wheel and rivetted into place. Some of the heat had trickled down into the sticky mouth. There is a deep valley of real sleep but this I had obviously failed to penetrate, flitting instead on the scorching uplands of an unsatisfactory nap.

I kept my eyelids firmly clamped down and reached for the switch controlling the electric light on my bedside table. It had always been my experience that suffused pink light via the eyelids was a gentle introduction to full illumination. The switch clicked but no pinkness hit the eyeballs. The bulb, I knew, was ancient and probably defective. Old-fashioned clear bulbs, however, can have their ruptured filaments rejoined under favourable conditions. One of these conditions, of course, is enough light to do the job and there remained therefore the problem of getting the first light gracefully onto the eyeball. I put my hand out towards the string controlling the laced folding slat-built blind of the nearby window and pulled briefly. The slats turned obediently and the eyeballs gratefully acknowledged the dull pinkish glow. I slowly lifted one lid and then the other and found that the level of illumination was tolerable. Next I groped with my hand on the bedside table for my glasses, placed them on my nose and ears and happily cut off the fuzzy edges of the objects before me. Blinking once or twice I shoved with my right index finger at the bridge of the glasses and they clicked finally into position.

I saw a group of girls at a distant corner. One was standing by her bicycle, two others tugged playfully at the handlebars and saddle respectively. Their schoolbooks, strapped into neat bundles, lay on the ground at their feet. Younger girls might have used schoolbags, the more studious small attaché cases. These were clearly, by their demeanour and accoutrements, girls in a slack school year between their intermediate and final examinations. The two were playing at preventing the girl with the bicycle from going home while she played at wanting to go.

The cause of this confrontation between this resistible force and that movable object came into view around a corner, a group of boys also equipped with standard issue strappings of books, one smoking as per programme. The boys stopped about thirty yards from the girls, whose playful battle redoubled its intensity momentarily, then ceased as they giggled, blushed and pointed, their hands making gestures narrower than the widths of their shoulders so that the boys should not notice. The boys dutifully failed to notice and continued a heedless conversation on football, cars and tennis-club hops. This new confrontation of resistible force and movable objects, the boys and the girls, soon sought resolution and the two groups broke up with a slow disentangling, the other two girls leaving the one with her bicycle, calling back to her over their shoulders obscure appointments and instructions; the boys spread equally slowly apart, drifting in amorphous groups of one or perhaps two or so in all directions.

One moved more slowly than the others and was available when the girl with the bicycle discovered a soft tyre. She postponed mounting her machine and took a pump from its metal moorings. She attached the rubber connection to valve and pump and manipulated the pump-piston industriously for a few strokes. There was a loud pop as the connection burst asunder. She was staring helplessly at her bicycle when the boy approached. They spoke briefly and came to the conclusion that the soft tyre was beyond remedy; the boy took the handlebars of the bike and began to wheel it away for her. She fell into step beside him and in making a show of attempting to wheel it herself found her hand resting in the comfortable crook of his elbow. Chatting and strolling, they too disappeared round the distant corner.

My spectacles, a heavy set with frames known to the trade as library frames, had slipped slightly down my nose and needed adjustment. I suspected that a fine film of overnight perspiration on the as yet unwashed face was the cause of the slippage and removed them, placing them carefully on the bedside table to leave my hands free for the skin-wiping. I immediately noticed the table lamp and remembered that I had as yet done nothing about the repair to the bulb.

I wiped the skin of the bridge of my nose and respectacled myself, unsocketed the bulb and set to work. Twin tendrils of fine-spun coiled filament pendulated sadly towards the lowered pot-belly bulge of the lamp. If these ends were to be made to touch and the current made again to flow through them so touching, they would fuse and a new if shorter filament would be there to enjoy some further hours of happy burning. Dexterously and slowly I swung the globe from side to side, watching the dangling filament ends as they swayed now nearer, now farther apart. A touch and their coiled adhesiveness of surface held them together. Then to manipulate the lamp-socket so that I could re-insert the bulb without shaking, then to click the switch and my poor eyeballs started back aghast into their own private sockets. The lamp was now brighter than rated, the surge of power through its shorter filament showering off slightly more quanticles per millisecond than your everyday hundred-watt job.

This would shorten the expectation of life of this poor little fila-ment but after all was I not giving it one crowded hour of glorious life if also an early age without a name? Suppose, indeed, I was to shorten the filament still further, would I not ultimately reach the shortest possible filament and the brightest possible light? Had I invented the photographic flash-bulb?

I switched off the light and allowed myself to sink back towards sleep but not quite so far as it. As my head rolled slightly, the side of my glasses, and the pillow, between them nipped my ear painfully and I jolted awake, the glasses slipping off.

The resultant fuzzed image of my room had several interesting features, more noticeable now that a brighter daylight was up and about in the street outside and finding its way through the slats of my blind. Near the foot of my bed, neatly screwed to the wall, was my mirror. Its rippled and bevelled edges gleamed opalescent with rims of red and green and soft interflowing fringes of yellow and blue, the discreet fractions remaining of the sun's morning delivery on its interstellar round.

Quintrillions of those quanticles, of brain-blistering miniatude, were being constantly disgorged from the sun, vomited out from its forced feeding of itself on itself. Exhausted after their journey, the pale few reached me. The rest had been lost on the way, snapped up by passing asteroids, planets, satellites and clouds, these last, when fed up with the whole operation, unloading the lot in gigantic discharges of hot white lightning, hell-flames from a heavenly body.

There was a flicker here of something reminding me of a dream in my fitful nap, a dimly-lit signpost pointing back the way I had come.

Not light nor fire nor thermal furnace. A street, dazzling golden yellow on one side, harsh black on the other, a jagged shadow's edge along the middle, the high sun glaring down over the scalloped edging of tiled roof. A blacker hole on the black side, doorway, dim stairway to an upper landing, a door to a gloomy room, light filtering from stairwell, corridor to a blacker hole, a windowless room, a bed. Through the wall, high above the bed, an oblong hole cut, to admit air from a passage which had in its turn no outlet to air or light. I am lying on the bed, eyes opened to the blackness, pupils distended catching the faint gleam of borrowed light. Suddenly a switch clicks, the oblong is illuminated, a greenish patch projects onto the farther wall. Voices, a foreign language, something about two people, the house being full. A cordial laugh. A throatier voice and another laugh. Silence, the switch clicks again, darkness. A girl's voice, dying away. I am in the shadow-bisected street again, flaring yellow sandstone walls under a glaring impartial sun.

Anyway, this was getting away from the morning's business; recollecting a dream is always difficult and always a waste of time; remembered imagined hopes and fears, the roughage of life's digestive tract, unnoticed by a body in the glow of health. I replaced my glasses. By now there was sufficient light available to and through my eyes to render the whole operation of mending the bulb a waste of time. I wondered what time it was. I reached out for my watch, lying obediently on the bedside table near the base of the lamp, but the lamp-work must have shifted it, for my fingers pushed it over the edge and it fell to the floor. Cosmic justice seemed to require that a slowly waking person be spared this series of petty annoyances; patience and resignation were called into play. I inverted my upper torso patiently and resignedly over the edge of the bed and groped below. With the head inverted the glasses slipped again, but this time upwards, so to speak, that is towards the forehead and away from the socketed nosebridge. My fingers came up with the watch-glass, sadly detached from its parent body. I brought it up close to my face to see if it at least had escaped damage and as I peered at it was surprised to see through it

A ragged column of young cyclists passing at moderate speed along a country road. The police bye-law requiring that cyclists travel no more than two abreast was not being strictly observed, although there was a tendency, no more, among the group to remain loosely formed into bi-sexual couples. The members of the group had a mean age of about eighteen years and seven months. The ratio of males to females was 1/1.23 recurring. As some of both the boys and the girls wore no socks, the number of socks per leg was 0.73. Most of the boys were wearing open-necked short-sleeved shirts of pastel colours and grey flannel trousers held tight at the ankle by clips designed to prevent the trouser-legs from fouling and being fouled by the driving-chains of the machines. Most of the girls were wearing blouses similar to the boys' shirts and cotton skirts of the style known as dirndl, a word in the German language denoting a garment worn by peasant girls in Bavaria and Austria, held tight by a broad band at the waist, flaring out slightly and extending just below the knee. These were in bright reds and blues and greens. One or two of the girls were wearing slacks like those of the majority of the boys. Two of the boys and one of the girls were wearing shorts, and these three, at the head of the column, were riding bicycles with handlebars curving sharply downwards and with the capacity to alter the ratio of movement of the crank-wheel to freewheel by a mechanism of the dérailleur type.

The posture, plump proportions and vigorous leg-action of this leading girl drew attention to her prominent bust, which, it appeared, was not supported with the rigidity held to be conventional. Change in public taste was to determine quite a different convention and girls of her age and endowment would affect a so-called natural look, all protuberances on the bust being left evident. It would be perfectly simple to devise a simulation of such protuberances on supports which could be worn by girls not endowed by nature with the features this 'look' required and I had no doubt ingenious manufacturers of ladies' undergarments had marketed such apparatus. Riding a bicycle with dropped handlebars might however require, for the sustaining of the simulation of the 'look' a mobility of the bust not allowed by protuberance-fitted supports.

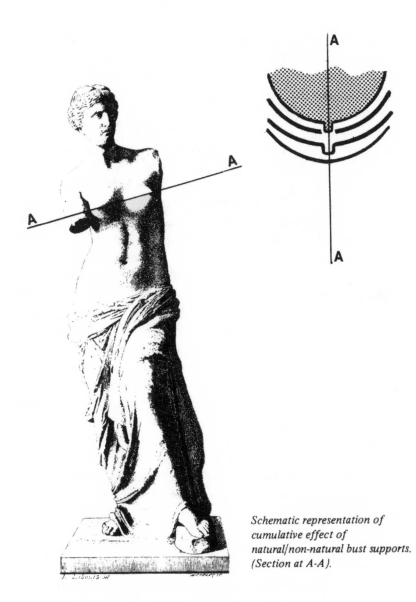

*Schematic representation of
cumulative effect of
natural/non-natural bust supports.
(Section at A-A).*

They would need, then, some attachment of light springing around the bases to impart this mobility; if this in its turn were found distressing by the wearer, the whole complicated support could be confined by one of the more conventional type—and, I suddenly realised, so on.

Each bicycle carried a small package strapped to its handlebars or clipped to a carrier mounted behind the saddle or, in the case of a few of the girls, in a light basket mounted on the handlebars and dangling dangerously over the front wheel. Each of these packets contained materials for a light lunch and a raincoat or cape of rubberised cotton.

The sun was shining with a watery bright yellowness proper to springtime, St. Patrick's Day or Easter Monday.

The one girl I recognised was roughly three-quarters way back through the column and losing place steadily. She was still having trouble with her soft tyre. Her next neighbour was a boy, the only other recognisable member of the group, and he kept even pace with her as her disability dropped her farther and farther back. In his face were mingled distress (at allowing himself to be passed out by fellow-cyclists, boys and girls, whom he regarded as his inferiors in prowess) and self-satisfaction with the protective role he had assumed towards his companion.

The road was poorly paved and each patch of loose repair metal made the girl wince a little as her soft tyre bumped across it. It was such bumping and her consequent slackening of speed which were gradually driving her back. Finally, she and her escort had reached the end of the column and the now-penultimate couple glanced back as they passed with grins and facetious comment.

At the next bump, she applied her brakes and stopped. Her companion stopped beside her and the column swung ahead round a corner into a black cavernous opening in a tunnel of overhanging trees and out of sight.

from

The Queen of the Prisons of Greece

Osman Lins

APRIL 26, 1974—Many times during the past year, so grim and empty, I have mentioned here my intention of occupying my spare time, of giving it meaning perhaps, by writing what Julia—Julia Marquezim Enone—always so private about herself, told me about her life, what I saw myself, and what I managed to find out later. How many nights have I spent looking at the few photographs she left behind, hearing the indistinct noise of traffic rising to this room, now empty? I know her notes, not always intelligible, almost by heart, as well as the recording of a conversation we had. Our daily chats are lost; I have managed to reconstruct only fragments of them, with a sharp sense of their irrecoverability.

Yes, I'd have a lot to say about her negligent and vulnerable ways, by which she seemed to suggest that she knew she was fragile and that, precisely because of this, she chose not to protect herself. I hesitate, limiting myself to a few brief and random comments about our life together.

At the same time, a vague idea that I don't want to record just yet has occurred to me during the last few days.

MAY 1—The idea returns and takes form. Instead of writing about the woman, why not write a study of the book, hers, which I read over and over again? It's a more reasonable and profitable alternative. After all, much of what I could say about Julia Enone would mean something only to me, like family pictures. Lacking the skill and the energy indispensable to the art of narrating, despite the attraction I feel toward fiction, I'd run the risk of suggesting but a pale shadow of my friend. Even if I scrupulously stuck to biography, without any fancy for incursions into the realm of the imaginary.

Dealing with the book presents obvious advantages. The text will keep me from getting tangled up in cherished memories and images, a labyrinth still to be mastered. Add, to the existence of the text, its nature. Texts: in principle, a universal gift. If we discuss them or shed light on them in any way—if we allow them to grow within us—we're working on a collective heritage.

In Julia Marquezim Enone's specific instance, the text to be enjoyed, it's true, hasn't been published. Because of this, its quality of public good (or evil) is debatable. Its existence limited to the original manuscript, and thus not even available to anyone who might want it, does it already belong to everybody?

MAY 2—I'm inclined to think that it does. The work, even if embryonic, concerns the collective being—us—whose substance informed it. Besides, those who deal with books must always bear in mind, and I believe that a return to this protracted period is not entirely unlikely, handwritten reproduction. Finally, the almost legendary book by Julia Marquezim Enone, in which sensitive and informed individuals recognize, painstakingly concealed, bold explorations, is circulating among several readers and people interested in the art of fiction, thanks to the sixty-five copies I myself ran off on an obsolete ditto machine.

One problem is still holding me back. Even accepting without reservations the public character of the literary work, even if unpublished; and the fact that this modest reproduction saves the book from complete anonymity, I'm still hesitant. What are the chances of finding a publisher for a study of a book almost unknown and inaccessible, for the time being, to the general reading public?

MAY 6—Let's hear, on the threshold of my possible study or mere commentary (who knows, on the other hand, where someone who's getting involved in this type of project is headed?), let's hear, half revealing and half enigmatic, the novelist's voice: "I've begun the book that was slowly taking form within me. Everything, at first, was preparation, expectation, plunder. And then? Then, it'll be Africa. As Rimbaud wrote, I will bury 'my imagination and my memories' and head 'for the port of misery.' " (Letter of 1/6/70 to the writer Hermilo Borba Filho.)

MAY 18—I discuss the project with A.B., professor at the Pontifical Catholic University, a man of great knowledge and somewhat ironic, who, since I'm fond of books, honors me with his esteem. What he tells me, even making allowances for some likely exaggeration, a tribute always to be paid to irony, worries me and, on the other hand, mitigates some of my apprehensions. A.B. tells me, with his shrewd ecclesiastical smile, what happens with some of his students and even well-known professors: if, for example, they know something about Madame de Volanges, de Danceny and the libertine Valmont, it's not because they have read *Dangerous Liaisons*, but because they're familiar with the explication published some eight years ago in the journal *Communications* of the novel by de Laclos, that connoisseur of fortifications and human weakness.

Nowadays, adds A.B., a publisher who brings out a literary study has a significant, eager audience, larger than the audience—real or possible—of the work analyzed, and who perhaps doesn't even deem it necessary to know it. He warns me, on the other hand, about the negative aspect of what might otherwise be an advantage: my intimacy with the author. The study of texts, claim the specialists nowadays, must ignore the hand that wrote them (charged, nevertheless, with history and obscure motives).

MAY 25—I see in the German magazine *Burda* an ad for Delft china, with this text in the midst of a selection of pitchers and other elegant wares: "Don't look at the bottom of the piece first. Avoid stereotypical reactions of admiration or trust. Delft products stand out for their beauty and quality."

Interestingly, this ad repeats what the Roman theorist Bruno Molisani says in a study of a Hugo poem ("Written upon the Glass of a Flemish Window"). There Molisani presents as something that was demonstrated, *a long time ago*, "the advantage, for the scholar, of not taking into account the author's name, which avoids stereotypical responses of admiration or trust."

Thus I think it's necessary to ask—still taking into account what A.B. told me—if I won't be wrong in disregarding an idea endorsed equally by literary studies and Delft faience ads, in dealing with Julia Marquezim Enone (or rather, with her book), I, who not only knew and know her name, but also hear it repeated so many times within myself, since we were lovers. Won't my work be doomed from the beginning to partiality, to failure, since I must fall prey, due to my past circumstances, to "stereotypical responses of admiration or trust"?

MAY 26—I could still ask: since the author doesn't exist, was I nobody's lover?

JUNE 3—I thought about it long and hard and decided not to back off in the face of decrees that—objective and laudable as they might be—lack knowledge in the widest sense of the word. Let's see. A mere letter can be better understood if compared to others—earlier and maybe even later ones—by the person who wrote it. Repetitions and changes can point to so many things! How can certain intentions and shades of meaning be translated if not by contrasting them, by setting them against a certain tradition, that is, an *authorship*? The same verses are not the same verses if they come from the epigonous Etienne Alane rather than Hugo. This is what Jorge Luis Borges, an Argentine who knows about these things, tells us, in his own way, in the story in which Ménard writes Cervantes' novel word for word. The style of the *Quixote*, natural in its first author, becomes archaic. The comparison of the two texts, says Borges, "is a revelation": Ménard has enriched the art of reading with a new technique, that of "deliberate anachronism and erroneous attributions." Borges suggests, among others, the experience of reading *The Imitation of Christ* attributed to Joyce.

Besides, since I'm far from being—and from the desire of being—an academician, why abide by rules? Let us forge ahead.

JUNE 10—Yes. Why submit to the trend predominant nowadays? I remember reading, in the *Almanac of Thought*, I suppose, or in some old issue of the *Lionhead Almanac*, what the Prussian Fontane wrote, not very elegantly perhaps, almost one hundred years ago: "Whenever it comes to the organization of the work, philosophers make inane judgments. They completely lack the organ to pick up the essential signals." "The opinion of a perceptive layman is always valuable; a professional aesthetician's is usually worthless."

Even though I probably lack finesse, at least I'm a layman. In any case, Fontane, I'm far from being your professional philosopher or aesthetician, I'm even far from the literary circles, which makes me lean in the opposite direction, that of the not entirely obtuse aficionados of the novel. It's in this capacity that I dream of discoursing about my dead friend's book, visited so many times and still so full of secrets.

JUNE 12—I knew the author, we lived together, I don't hide the fact that I loved her. Love doesn't necessarily mean blindness and deception. The widower Middleton Murry is not wrong when he presents his Katherine Mansfield's *Journal*. My love for Julia Marquezim Enone will inevitably show in some pages—maybe even in all of them. Even if this fact were to lessen the study's lucidity and impartiality, and I trust that no injustice will be done to either, lucidity or impartiality, I have trouble admitting that this would invalidate my commentary. For which inflexible law would oblige us to conceal our ardor before a work of art as shameful? Just how coherent is it to willingly block out part of our mental faculties with regard to this object that appeals to the totality of our being in order to talk about it with a detachment it does not aspire to by its own nature?

I won't fall into the error of "discussing the poet and not the poem," by which I'll avoid lucid Pound's classic criticism. But I won't demand of myself voluntary mutilations in the study I plan either. Never. Only my restraint, if I don't overcome it, and a certain tact, will limit the frankness of the work—an analysis or, who knows, just a memoir—from which an elegiac note will certainly not be missing.

Oh Julia, who, in spite of everything, I won't call mine, since you were always headed for some mysterious region, invisible and uncharted!

JULY 15—Part of the month of June and half of the school vacation have been spent making plans for my essay over and over again, without choosing one: all of them, with their brackets and subdivisions, imitate the charts—so useful, after all—with which the Linnaeuses of this world try to order nature. I think today I found a solution.

Every literary essay, following a convention consolidated by authority, evokes a hidden narrator. Unavoidable, in both cases, the so called *personal* discourse—which clarifies the circumstances of the utterance. The essayist never addresses us in a definite time or place: atemporal and somewhat abstract, he only reveals to us, by the artifice of a text that in a way conceals him and thus deceives us, his readings (always commendable) and his ideas (never unfinished).

I will take another direction. I want an essay in which, abdicating immunity to time, and, as a consequence, immunity to surprise and hesitation, I will establish with the reader—or accomplice—a more honest relationship. What other option stands out more naturally than the diary in this case? This way I will follow the progress and the turns in the questions that occur to me day by day.

My disadvantage in comparison with the authors of fictional diaries imagined by Goethe (*Werther*), Machado de Assis (*Aires' Memorial*), Gide (*The Pastoral Symphony*) is apparent. They all dealt with women—Charlotte, Fidélia, Gertrude—whereas my hero is just a book. At least the not insignificant circumstance that the book and I are real is in my favor.

Let's therefore go on to my essay, half intimate, half public, confidential, a book that is to be composed slowly and imprinted with the passing of days.

May I not irrevocably fall prey to solitude by trying to elude it. May I not have to complain, like Goethe: "here, as well as everywhere else, I always find both what I am seeking and what I am running from."

JULY 17—Nietzsche writes, I don't remember where, that a philosophy is always the expression of a personality. Julia Marquezim Enone wasn't tainted by the fierce need to astonish that afflicts most contemporary artists. Discreet, cultivating an uncommon kind of elegance, an intimate elegance, invisible, full of modesty, she rejected all forms of ostentation—a glaring proof of arrogance, in her view. Obvious originality pained her.

How to solve the problem, if she, as honest as someone lacking imagination—she, who incessantly enlarged the world—would never stoop to taking the beaten path; if she looked at writing and natural things from a perspective not at all trivial; if she couldn't hide her ineptitude when faced with what's established?

She chose, and her personality thus engendered, if not a philosophy, a poetics, a novel apparently following closely the models of the past. Going deliberately against the most widespread and respected dogma of modern fiction, which looks askance at the plot, she structured *The Queen of the Prisons of Greece* around an uninterrupted chain of events centering on Maria de França, a moneyless mulatto heroine lost in the stairways, corridors and halls of the social welfare bureaucracy, where she struggles to obtain a certain benefit.

When everything would lead us to believe that we have a conventional work in our hands, the opposite happens. And it does so because the narrator strives to conceal her inventions. If this trait, fundamental in the author, escapes us, we will assess the book incorrectly. Discovering in it what is elaborate and personal—and my discoveries in this area, until now discontinuous and undisciplined, barely allow a glimpse of all those hidden lodes—will be the main goal of my essay, or whatever else it might be called.

JULY 18—". . . when she noticed a very curious appearance in the air: it puzzled her very much at first, but after watching it a minute or two she made it out to be a grin, and she said to herself: 'It's the Cheshire-Cat: now I shall have somebody to talk to.' "—Lewis Carroll, *Alice in Wonderland*, chap. 8.

JULY 19—What's the use of a book's synopsis? A superficial practice, it spreads and resurrects the common idea according to which the story *is* the novel, not one of its aspects, among those that illustrate the art of narrating the least. Imagining desires, mishaps, reversals of fortune, capitulations, death or triumph, pertains to invention in its raw state. The novelist is born by the act of arranging these events and elaborating a language that could either reflect them or simply make use of them to exist.

Here, however, summarizing the facts narrated in the book we are to discuss is indispensable. Since it hasn't been published yet (I'll explain the reasons for this in due time), my readers would be left in the position of someone who finds himself at a debate he knows nothing about. Without further delay—I don't want to be the target of Montaigne's criticism of Cicero, whose speeches, he said, swollen with preparatory remarks as they are, "languish around the pot"—I will therefore return to the novel and summarize it, so as to convey, without Propp's assistance—bound by other commitments—as faithful an idea as possible of the heroine's banal adventures, adventures which repetitions and variations turn into a nightmare. I will alter the order of the original where necessary.

Translation by Adria Frizzi

from

A Short Rhetoric for Leaving the Family

Peter Dimock

Delivery, with good reason, has been called the most important part of rhetoric. Delivery is the graceful regulation of voice, demeanor, and gesture—a way of creating presence out of air. Only a practiced rule of rhetoric will allow you to retain for immediate use words, ideas, events, and their arrangement and to pass them on effectively as speech, suitable again for memory. Only rhetoric and its history have a very close relationship to private and public affairs and can ensure the safe protection of oneself and one's friends. Delivery may be divided into two parts, gesture and sound. Quality of voice should be perfected with respect to flexibility, volume, and stability. Do not rely upon the family's privilege and exemption when you speak. It helps if you imagine some sound for the feel of careful speech leaving the warm opening of the mouth.

Sharp exclamation injures the voice and likewise jars the hearer. It imparts awkwardness to the occasion, belonging more to the world of feminine outcry than to the dignity of forceful speech. Flexibility of voice has three aspects: the conversational tone, the tone of debate, and the tone of amplification. The latter's function is to rouse the hearer to anger or pity.

For the narrative, conversational tone, varied intonations are necessary so that we seem to recount everything just as it took place. Learn to do good. Memorize what has been said in order to know what is true. Adopt a new and easy sweetness of tone for an idea of it afterwards. Invent some pleasured speech to recount an event of family history accurately.

Your delivery should be fairly rapid when you narrate that which was done with force, slower when you speak of things done in a more leisurely fashion. If in the statement of facts there occur any declarations, demands, replies, or exclamations of astonishment, you should give careful attention to expressing with your voice the feelings and thoughts of the personage your speech concerns.

It is one thing to acquire the art of direct address and another to make use of it through the art of delivery.

Do not use up the brilliance of the voice in one loud outburst. A calm tone in the introduction is useful for the voice's stability.

We cannot choose our fathers, but it is our responsibility to imagine them. Sharp exclamation injures the voice and likewise jars the hearer.

The conversational tone is divided into four aspects: the dignified, the explicative, the narrative, and the facetious. The narrative is to be cultivated so as to impart to your listener a convincing account of events that have occurred or might have occurred. The tone of amplification is divided into two aspects: the hortatory and the pathetic. The hortatory is to be used to emphasize a fault or to incite a listener's indignation. The pathetic is to be used to amplify misfortune and thereby to win over a listener to pity. The tone of debate is divided into the sustained and the broken.

For the dignified conversational tone you will need to use the full throat, but employ the calmest, most subdued voice possible, without stooping to histrionics.

Without empire and the pleasured will, what possible fulfillment for the citizen? Some sound for the pleasure of rule in this New World. For the broken tone of debate, shoot out one arm laterally very quickly, pace up and down, stop and stomp the right foot occasionally. Peer about you with a piercing, fixed, and determined expression. As if speech, or fire, could take the place of burning skin and make its discarded pleasure sing.

For the pathetic tone of amplification, it is appropriate to slap your thigh and strike your head with your open hand, alternating these gestures with the resigned calmness of deliberate movements, yet with a disturbed expression on your face. I do realize, of course, what a difficult task I have undertaken here—to convey in writing the movements of the body and the sound of the voice speaking its pleasure.

Father's health has worsened over the past few days. Everything grows less familiar to him. His confusion seems limitless. Some days are better, a little, than others. There is now very little time, the doctors think. Dead family members come back to him in the hall of a house he remembers from childhood that I have never seen. I have held onto this letter probably for too long. I will make copies soon and send them, one for each of you, and one to Elizabeth. The original I will keep in case either of you, or I myself, should ever require it. Everyone, he once said, owed, when required, the state a life. The best men, he thought, had the responsibility to rule without restraint. He committed crimes against humanity. This is documented. I have been a disloyal son and committed treason, the evidence could be made to show.

The actual event can lose its independent value. An abstruse art of allegorical exegesis is born whenever this occurs. Invent some speech for the pleasured man's burning.

As you become practiced in this method, remember to allow yourselves freedom to depart from adherence to its exact prescriptions.

Remember that the windpipe is injured when filled suddenly with violent outbursts of sound and that it is rested by silence. Do not hesitate to employ long pauses, especially when you are using the conversational tone. Toward the close of speaking, it is perfectly proper to deliver long passages of sound in one unbroken breath. The throat is warm and the voice has been restored by your use of all the tones of address.

I recommend that you refrain from committing to writing anything you do not intend to memorize and use in some manner of direct address. Your body should be unencumbered when you speak. Good men, he said, should rule. Anything else, history showed, was abdication of responsibility and an invitation to the worst, who are always present. Evil was limitless. The doctrine of natural depravity, he maintained, was empirically verified and a precious inheritance.

Unlike stability of voice, flexibility depends entirely upon adherence to rhetorical rules. The tone of conversation should be relaxed and close to common speech. The tone of debate should be excited, equally suited as it is to vehement proof and vehement refutation. There will need to be some speech afterwards for the way empire penetrates the skin.

Because I do not know when I will be back East again, I have been to check on the condition of Father's house in Maine to see if it needed anything. While I was there, I walked the old logging road he always used to walk. A little way in, I found the dessicated remnants of a young porcupine lying in the sun, and I suddenly knew I was free to release my argument. I don't pretend to understand why seeing the ground through its blackened strips of skin made me eloquent, but it did: some careful speech for an idea of him.

Preserve in memory the evidence against him, and do not neglect the pleasured uses of invective. General, as you know, I and your father are hopelessly estranged. I would like to think that I wish him no ill.

When discussing delivery, it is necessary to pay close attention to the body's physical movements. The body must move so as to increase the plausibility of what you say. Be careful not to go too far either on the side of elegance or vulgarity. Remember you are not an actor on stage. For the conversational, explicative tone, lean forward and bring your face as close to your listeners as possible, since this is the way to prove something conclusively or get someone to act on what you say. For the pathetic tone of amplification, combine slow and graceful—sometimes halting—gestures with a sad and wounded expression and a calm, even tone of voice for the strongest effect.

Father signed the memorandum authorizing offensive action on the part of U.S. troops in the President's name, 6 April 1965. I am confident now of my trust in you especially because I am not aware of having omitted any of the rules of rhetoric from what I have written here. If I do not hear from either of you, I will understand. Silence, according to this method, is also a way of speaking. And if you want to ask me in person what it is I have been doing all these years, perhaps I will ask your permission to say aloud a little of what I have written here. I will begin anywhere and proceed for as long as I can manage from memory.

from

Things in the Night

Mati Unt

My Dear, I feel I owe you an explanation.

First, I have to admit that I have always been interested in electricity. For the most part I've kept my passion a secret, but have not always been able to avoid temptation, so one or two of my plans have leaked out to the general public.

Some ten years ago or so, I felt that I had to restrict myself by some kind of vow, which may sound rather intriguing, and so I began issuing IOUs. I announced that I was writing a book on electricity. Of course, people wanted to know immediately what kind of book I had in mind. I said: One in the most general sense of the word. I was met with sympathetic stares, the kind you get if you say you are going to write a novel about Life, which is too broad a concept, or white mice, which is too narrow. I wasn't taken seriously, and people were right, of course, because I didn't have any idea what I really wanted either. Sometimes I suspected that I'd become pretentious, or having grown fed up with long novels about marriage, that I was simply lazy. Who writes about electricity, anyway? You might as well tell people: I'm going to write about a flowing river.

I cannot conceal the fact that one of Francis Ponge's compositions appeals to me, one that was commissioned by some electric company. With Professor Ivask's help, I managed to find it in a bilingual collection:

> *De l'electricité telle qu'actuellement a la sensibilité de l'homme elle se propose, aucune grande chose dans l'ordre poétique, après tout, n'est sortie non plus. Ce retard, chez les architectes comme les poètes, ne tiendrait-il pas aux mêmes causes? Les architectes comme les poetes, sont des artistes. En tant que tels, ils voient les choses dans 'l'eternité plus que dans le temporel. Pratiquement, ils se défient de la mode. Je parle des meilleurs d'entre eux.*

(With electricity, as it is now available to man, a truly great thing has yet to be achieved, at least so far as poetry is concerned. Couldn't this lag among architects and poets be due to the same cause? Architects, like poets, are artists. As such, they see things in eternity more than in the temporal. In practical terms, they defy fashion. I speak of the best of them.)

I tried not to resort immediately to abstractions, tried not to make that *grande chose dans l'ordre poétique*. I wanted to start with memories, entirely personal ones. For instance, that around 1958, when I was alone in Aunt Ida's apartment where, on the wall, next to a copy of a Kuindzhi painting, or rather, between the painting and the window, there hung a table lamp. Yes, that's what I mean, a table lamp, except for the fact that it was hanging on the wall. It had a metal frame and what I understood to be decoration, at any rate some kind of bas-relief or veining. I remember that the shade had been burned from its original yellow to brown as if too strong a bulb had been put in the lamp. So there I was, standing at the window—I clearly remember the thick net curtains, which almost entirely obscured the view of Teguri Street (trees and a fence—or only trees—and other things, of course). What I was thinking, what led me to do what I did, is something I do not know. I perhaps had some boyish thoughts in my head, I was after all a boy at the time, and viewed life through optimistic eyes, at least I think so, though I don't remember exactly, but at that age there isn't much choice of torments, I mean to say you can choose between them, but the choice isn't difficult to make, mostly because of a lack of painful experiences. In a word, whether I was in a situation where I did the choosing or not, I tried to take the lamp down from the wall. It was daytime, that I'm pretty sure of, and I believe that the lamp wasn't switched on. I presumably wanted to take a closer look at it, or perhaps something had rolled under the sofa. At any rate, the electricity suddenly caused my hand to seize the lamp stand tightly. I don't remember any more, except, of course, my surprise. I didn't regain consciousness until the lamp had fallen on the sofa, though I remained standing where I was. I had clearly got my hand loose somehow, or maybe the current was cut. But what would have happened otherwise?

That is only one small instance of my encounters with electricity, and not even the most important one, because I had totally forgotten it and only remembered when I began to put together my personal memories of electricity. Especially the personal ones, was what I was thinking, as I had begun to suspect a good while earlier that electrical energy can have a great effect on the human organism and the subconscious.

Sometimes I would sit in the room and try to identify the effect of electrical waves. There had to be such waves all around me because I was surrounded by cables that ran in conduits through the walls, hung above me, and wound their way across the floor. It was difficult to listen to the radio in the bedroom. There was significant interference on the mid-range of the band. What else could cause this but electrical waves?

Waves all around me? What could be more intriguing? Was this a hidden enemy or friend?

I can't forget that I grew up at a time when science was both made mysterious and anthropomorphized. I remember various book titles: *Taming Water! Mobilizing the Forest! Machines Proceed to the Field of Victory!* There had to be one about waves. *Unseen Waves! Electricity as Epic Hero!*

I wanted to do some research. Where should I begin? I remember that Jay Gatsby used to learn the principles of electricity between 7:15 and 8:15 in the morning. Before these, exercises with dumbbells; afterwards, work. Quite. I had to start investigating, as I thought at the time, not confine myself to pathos (Whitman: *I sing the body electric*).

We are clearly dealing with enormous power. Richard Feynman offers this unworldly example in one of his lectures. Let us assume that we are standing next to one another as we are doing right now, at arms' length. If your body or mine suddenly were to gain one percent more electrons than protons, an electrical charge would be set up between us that could move a mass the size of the Earth. That also shows, by the way, how finely tuned matter is.

But I am getting off the point. Better for me to talk about my own experiments.

.   .   .

Afterwards, we were again driving through fields, in a strange car, among strangers.

The grain was growing lush, the rain was on its way, the grain at risk as always.

The cemetery was left behind, including all the flesh, blood, skin, and bones.

The grain was bright, swayed, billowed. Yes, just like the sea, only white.

The grain was bright, the sky dark.

The sky is darker than the earth, I've known that since I was a child. In winter the sky is darker than the snow. In summer the sky is darker than the grain.

I said to You:

"Look."

"What?" You asked. "Where?"

"There, there, quick, look."

You looked but no doubt saw nothing.

I pointed with my finger. You looked.

Then You turned to me.

"It was just as if there were little eyes out there in the rye, little ones, black ones. Am I right?"

"You're right, my dear."

The rye ended, now there were potato fields, then came the beets, then potatoes again.

There were trends in those years, ones that did not of course leave me untouched either, though I tried to let them affect me as little as possible. There were various trends and a number of them really did affect me directly. I noticed phenomena around me that were hard to define, but they got mixed in with things I had loved for years. I had, for example, been involved for years with the fate of the world. I now felt a slight nausea when the thought struck me that I was responsible for everything. That kind of metamorphosis was calling forth reality, everyday life that was of course as opaque as always, like a Mayan veil covering everything, myself included. I was walking as if in a thick fog, though the sky was clear. Later on, I read in the papers that the world and mankind had begun to decline and the end was near. Lethargy started to appear everywhere. So we felt we all had something in common. In its own way, it was a pity that we weren't being honest with one another, weren't sharing our impressions. On the other hand, it was good that we didn't understand why we were happy. Now, my dear, I know. We no longer needed to develop or evolve in any way. We were doomed to die and we were no longer linked to life by any kind of responsibility. We could be as free as the pigs who ran in the fields. Those were beautiful years, beautiful autumn days.

Translation by Eric Dickens

Book Reviews

László Krasznahorkai. *War and War*. Trans. George Szirtes. New Directions, 2006. 279 pp. Paper: $16.95.

Written in 1999, *War and War* is a bitter but playful parable for our world of permanent emergency: the story of a Hungarian archivist and hypochondriac named Korin, who discovers a manuscript hidden in the file of an otherwise unremarkable local family. This text—about a group of philosophically inclined strangers who arrive, again and again, throughout history, to admire a particular civilization before catastrophe erases it—so impresses poor Korin that he decides to sell everything he owns and travel to New York, the center of the world, to upload the book to the Internet (which he laughably believes will preserve his find forever). This quest, which Korin hopes to cap by killing himself, is reported piecemeal in chapters that are only one sentence long—from a few hundred words to several pages each. Elongated to the point of parody, and then further—finally achieving a sense of breathless compression that brevity alone could never accomplish—these blocks of text inch the novel forward by letting us eavesdrop on Korin telling various more or less disinterested, sometimes hostile, bystanders about his holy mission, giving the reader a sense of absolute stasis and breathless motion simultaneously: things never *happen* in this world, but always *have been happening*, seething and chaotic, between the "sentences" that struggle to keep us clued in, third-hand, to Korin's progress towards erasure. *War and War* is only the second Krasznahorkai novel to be translated into English, following *The Melancholy of Resistance* (also translated by George Szirtes—excellent with everything but cursing and computers—and brought out in America by New Directions six years ago), but even with just this meager evidence to hand, the power and substance of Krasznahorkai's prose, its quality both of familiarity (qua Thomas Bernhard) and fundamental peculiarity (those epic, sinuous, mocking, endlessly associative sentences), is such that his Anglophone readers are bound to feel that he's already a major force—and long established—in our literature: this era's standard-bearer for a tradition of transience, skepticism, and negation. This feeling is well justified—let's hope the rest of Krasznahorkai's untranslated oeuvre is forthcoming in English, and soon. [Jeremy M. Davies]

Julien Gracq. *Reading Writing*. Trans. Jeanine Herman. Turtle Point Press, 2006. 376 pp. Paper: $17.50.

"There is no organized discourse for intimate communication with a book," writes Julien Gracq. This sentiment is echoed throughout *Reading Writing*, an impressionistic, aphoristic, and deeply personal collection of essays on reading, writing and the arts. Gracq eschews working within the kinds of theoretical frames of reference so common in academic criticism these days in favor of following his intuitions wherever they lead, often to brilliant ends. His central obsession is nineteenth-century French literature, and his essay on Stendahl, Balzac, Flaubert, and Zola—the book's longest and best—is a passionate examination of the inner workings of their styles: "Flaubert's cadences—how doleful and monotonous! Sometimes, it's true, the sentence will start with a lively movement, but it is like a happy stream rushing to throw itself inevitably into a pond." Gracq's main register is metaphoric, and his sentences have a powerhouse quality about them: "Every time I reopen *Remembrance of Things Past*, I am more sensitive to the primacy of the material over the architecture, of the cellular tissue over the differentiated organ, of the density of the verbal flow over the free air of space accorded to the characters, of the concrete duration of reading over the figurative time of the narrative." His poetics is rooted in the synapses: "What I want from a literary critic—and what is rarely given—is for the critic to tell me, better than I could do myself, why reading a book gives me a pleasure that cannot be replaced." In an essay on literary movements, Gracq barely shields his contempt for the stock-market-like fluctuations of popular reputation; he abhors the "extra-literary factors" ("physical or moral prestige, membership in a group, friends, lovers, a sparkling biography, a historical or political role") that often determine an author's importance. He sees in Victor Hugo a counterweight to this phenomenon, calling him "the first literary person to rise to the level of one of this world's powerful by the exclusive virtue of his pen, without ever trading literary glory for other values." Gracq possesses more than a bit of such single-mindedness. The value of *Reading Writing* lies in his autonomous vision of literary landscapes. [Tayt Harlin]

J. K. Huysmans. *Downstream*. Trans. Robert Baldick. Turtle Point Press, 2005. 69 pp. Paper: $10.95.

Published in 1882 as "Jean Folantin," *Downstream* (*A vau-l'eau*) first appeared in English in 1927. The title informs us that such is the direction in which the depressed drift—in this case, M. Folantin, a dyspeptic Parisian clerk self-deprived of family, fun and future, who spends his days copying documents and his evenings searching for a palatable meal. As his lonely days lethargically pass by, Folantin finds brief diversion in the redecorating of his lodgings and the discovery of a patisserie that delivers. Otherwise, everything bores him: his job, the theater, his acquaintances, women, the very streets he walks. Overwhelmed by "the immense weariness of an aimless, hopeless existence," Folantin brightens upon occasion only when he discovers a new quack tonic that promises to remedy his digestive woes—a problem that stems more from the staleness of his life and his sour view of the world than from the "appalling cheese" and "leathery beef" he consumes in one greasy *cuiller* after another. Here, for instance, is his impression of his fellow diners during yet another disappointing meal: "The seats were filled by all the Southern peoples, spitting, sprawling and bellowing; the entire population of Provence, Gascogny and Lanquedoc . . . roaring with laughter like madmen, making epileptic gestures and mouthing ear-splitting fragments of mutilated sentences." An autobiographical exercise that condenses some of the material in the earlier *Living Together (En Ménage)*, *Downstream* offers an excellent brief introduction to the comic/sad naturalism that Huysmans was writing just a few years prior to *A rebours* and *Là-bas*. This new translation, by Huysmans's biographer, captures the dreary tedium of Folantin's days with greater clarity than the earlier English version, without itself becoming dismal or monotonous. [Brooke Horvath]

Aharon Appelfeld. *Katerina*. Trans. Jeffrey M. Green. Schocken Books, 2006. 212 pp. Paper: $13.00.

The Holocaust looms about Aharon Appelfeld's fiction. For forty years, Appelfeld, himself deported to the camps when he was only eight, has confronted its forbidding obscenity, but indirectly—tales of family members whose relatives did not survive, of those whose idyllic days dwindle away even as the catastrophe relentlessly approaches, or of those haunted by their fortunate survival. In *Katerina*, a Christian farmgirl flees an abusive father in late 1880s Ukraine. She becomes a housekeeper for a Jewish family and comes to appreciate the rich traditions of the Jewish faith—its compassion, its magnificent spirituality, and its dignified acceptance of suffering. Given the angry intolerance in Europe between the wars, Katerina is warned to avoid Jews (she takes a Jewish lover and elects to raise their son as a Jew). In a pitch perfect first-person plainsong, Katerina recounts how the Jews who befriend her—gifted, humane, generous—die one after the other in acts of ethnic violence. When a drunk, intent on raping her, kills her baby in front of her, Katerina does what the Jews will not: she fights back. She dispatches him with a knife and is sentenced to life. There, in a prison that borders a railroad line, Katerina watches the grim procession of cattle cars heading to the concentration camps while the prisoners cheer. When Katerina escapes as the Nazi regime collapses, she returns, nearly eighty, to her village in a post-war world she fears now emptied of Jews—but she is determined to bear witness (Jews, she fears, live only in her heart). Given the sorry evidence of humanity's mayhem, only her unshakable faith reassures her. Without hysteria, without preaching, *Katerina*'s unadorned parabolic starkness reminds a twenty-first century world, itself growing distant from the calamity of the Holocaust, of the deep outrage it still inflicts. [Joseph Dewey]

Hermann Ungar. *Boys & Murderers*. Preface by Thomas Mann. Twisted Spoon Press, 2006. 252 pp. Paper: $15.00.

If American readers know Czech writer Ungar at all they are likely to know *The Maimed*, a beautiful and grotesque short novel that reads like the verbal equivalent of an Otto Dix drawing. Ungar, who wrote in the 1920s and was dead at age 36 by 1929, was a contemporary of Kafka's, an expressionist who, despite the excellence of his slim body of work, is largely unknown today. *Boys & Murderers* combines two of Ungar's books of shorter fiction plus a series of uncollected stories. The first book, "Boys & Murderers," consists of two novellas. One, "A Man and a Maid," chronicles an orphan's perverse obsession with the maid of his hospice, an obsession that becomes the defining principle of his life. "Story of a Murder," the second novella, explores the circumstances that lead a young man to murder the person most likely to be a friend and support him instead of killing his tormentors. These both show Ungar at his best, interested in the darker, distorted stretches of the human mind, willing to look unflinchingly and quite unforgivingly at humanity. The second book, "Colbert's Journey," was posthumously published and consists of nine shorter pieces, the longest around 20 pages, most less than half a dozen pages. The stories here are well written but give less of the flavor of Ungar's particular obsessions, though pieces like "The Secret War" manage to unearth human frailty very quickly and expertly. "Colbert's Journey," which charts in painful detail an unwitting man's destruction at the hands of his servant, is also quite good. The final section of six uncollected stories consists of work that seems more occasional. Though these stories are interesting they are rarely compelling. Still, taken as a whole, there is much to be admired in this volume, and much in keeping with Ungar's novels. *Boys & Murderers* strengthens the case for Ungar being an unjustly neglected writer. [Brian Evenson]

Helene Cixous. *The Day I Wasn't There*. Trans. Beverly Bie Brahic. Northwestern University Press, 2006. 120 pp. Paper: $19.95.

The title refers to the day Cixous' son dies, a Down's Syndrome baby (Cixous uses the older term *mongolism*), but it also underlines a life lived, that of the German-Jewish Cixous family transplanted to Algeria—no longer German, never accepted by the French or Arabs, nowhere at home, always "passing by, in passance . . . I saw that I would never arrive in France." Although Cixous identifies with Arabs, they will not let her be one. It is, she writes, "My Algeriance." Though the book circles around the day her son dies, discussions with her mother and doctor brother about how it happened—could he have been saved? Why wasn't she consulted? (Her mother tells her it's better he die.) Where was she?—increasingly identify Cixous' life with that of her son. "Overnight I ceased writing and I began a mongolian life"; that is to say, it was no longer possible for her to write in a conventional way—her life precludes it—and she thus had to find a way that others would find strange, outside the pale, mongolian—be described as the medical profession describes her son. "A writer," Theodor Adorno argues, "will find that the more precisely, conscientiously, appropriately he expresses himself the more obscure the literary result is thought, whereas a loose and irresponsible formulation is at once rewarded with a certain understanding." Cixous tracks down her son's grave and removes some of his remains to take with her. "What hadn't been given to me, I had taken." It is a statement of how a writer comes to core, or in terms of family, closure. "For a man who no longer has a homeland"—again it is Adorno, a German Jew writing in exile from America—"writing becomes a place to live." [Robert Buckeye]

Michel Houellebecq. *The Possibility of an Island*. Trans. Gavin Bowd. Knopf, 2006. 337 pp. $24.95.

Like its acclaimed predecessor *The Elementary Particles* (1998), Michel Houellebecq's latest novel projects an evolutionary future in which *homo sapiens* have been surpassed. The seeds of that future lie in a series of events witnessed by Daniel—a misanthropic, iconoclastic, and world-famous comedian on the brink of old age and sexual decline. As with Houellebecq's other narrators, Daniel's story reads like a *reductio ad absurdum* of Schopenhauer, Darwin, and Freud. Life for him revolves entirely around sex: "All energy is of a sexual nature, not mainly, but exclusively, and when the animal is no longer good for reproducing, it is absolutely no longer good for anything; it is the same for men." When he gets involved with a new-age religious cult called the Elohimites, the self-extinction of humanity begins. But Daniel's story lives on for two more millennia, sustained in the minds of his cloned "neohuman" successors and co-narrators, Daniel24 and Daniel25. This science fiction premise is more imaginative and well-developed than that of *The Elementary Particles*, but Houellebecq devotes most of his attention to the original Daniel's all too human quest for happiness. As in *Platform* (2001), the laws of existence are ruthlessly simple: once you lose the power to attract lithe young bodies and harvest pleasure from them, life is no longer worth living, and old age promises only "the unbearable pain of emotional isolation." While the neohumans manage to overcome the torments that accompany sex and mortality, in the process they sacrifice the pleasures and the passions. In the novel's visionary final scenes, Daniel25 sets out on an epic quest to discover whether this evolutionary trade-off was worth it. In general, Houellebecq's fiction may sometimes strive too hard to shock, and its sexist, intolerant, and nihilistic overtones may put some readers off. But like Daniel's comic routines, it never fails to deliver galvanizing jolts of grotesque honesty. [Thomas Hove]

James Chapman. *Stet*. Fugue State Press, 2006. 336 pp. Paper: $16.00.

"All of history comes about because of certain people's abilities to change the subject," writes James Chapman in his urgent new novel, *Stet*. If history is a red herring, then Chapman's red herring is Soviet, but no novel has ever been as powerfully targeted by analogy at the American artist today. The expression "Stet" itself, the name of the novel's protagonist, is a proofreader's mark indicating "Leave it the way it was before change was erroneously suggested." That seems precisely to be what Chapman is getting at in this pseudo-Russian novel. Sure, America won the Cold War, but what have we lost in the process? Is the price Russian culture? Is the worldwide replacement of Gogol, Dostoevsky and Shostakovich with *Jack-*

ass and Jessica Simpson really the direction international culture should be headed? How much further must we debase art before we reclaim loftier ambitions? Chapman revisits one of his favorite themes, the artist's role in a world hostile to art, elucidated brilliantly in *In Candyland It's Cool to Feed on Your Friends* (1997). In *Stet*, Chapman continues this examination, but of course the extinction of art looms larger now. Our undoing of great art is analogous to the undoing of Soviet filmmaker Stet, whose story in some ways resembles Shostakovich's and in other ways any serious artist's. Was oppression by Soviet censors really any worse than the systematic neglect of artistic originality? Did communism produce worse art than our cookie-cutter capitalism has? Why have we surrendered art to corporations? Chapman's novel illustrates what we've abandoned, and his lush, imagistic, euphonic prose is a sensory delight while it addresses the deepest, most significant matters of human nature. It is a novel that everyone should read, but *Fear Factor*'s on. [Eckhard Gerdes]

Rebecca Lee. *The City Is a Rising Tide*. Simon & Schuster, 2006. 200 pp. $21.00.

The City Is a Rising Tide is a slim debut novel that took Rebecca Lee ten years to hone into its final form. The result of this obviously painstaking effort is a marvel of concision, with a complex story that deftly hopscotches from China to North Carolina to the plains of middle Canada as a sympathetic but fundamentally untrustworthy narrator relates her experiences working for a nonprofit organization that's attempting to build a spiritual retreat along the Yangtze River. Given the impending damming of the river, she knows the project to be a futile effort, just as her one-sidedly romantic relationship with her boss is, but she drifts along with both. Despite her apparent passivity, she becomes the central figure in a series of financial, legal and even cinematic crises, the ultimate resolution of which will occur beyond the final pages. Even as the settings vary, the emphatic center of the book is New York. The city is lit with nostalgic 1990s warmth (how much of that nostalgia is intentional and how much is just inevitable in any writing that references the period before 9/11?) that makes this melancholic comedy of manners as much a love letter to Manhattan as Todd McEwen's underrated *Who Sleeps With Katz*. This shouldn't suggest that Lee's concerns are parochial, though. *Rising Tide* treats an entire network of personal, political, sociological, aesthetic and theological topics, becoming in effect a miniature systems novel—Joseph McElroy's *Women and Men* writ small. It's surprising how many ingredients are combined into something that initially feels so light. One character says, "A person can carry a whole world of ideas and associations and plotlines, don't you see?" Rebecca Lee proves a person can carry that world conveniently in a pocket. [James Crossley]

Marguerite Duras. *Yann Andrea Steiner*. Trans. Mark Polizzotti. Archipelago Books. 2006. 140 pp. Paper: $15.00.

Yann Andrea Steiner is a mélange of three stories: 1) the beach and sky, the grey-eyed child, his counselor, the story of the shark Duras had included in *L'Été 80*, a diary of her life in Trouville; 2) her meeting with Yann Andrea, the young man who was to be her companion and love the last years of her life; 3) the story of Theodora Katz, based on a drawing a Jewish woman (a friend of Duras's) discovered in Auschwitz, which Duras never completed. "I thought I had burned my novel, Theodora," Duras says. "I found it, unfinished and unfinishable, in my blue armoires."

"One never knows a story before it's written," Duras notes, but *Yann Andrea Steiner* is less a story than autobiography, less autobiography than hope. "I'm going from me to me," she comments about the book, and in it she visits (and revisits) talismanic sites in her life: love and desire; death; the Holocaust; sky, water and beach; solitude. Only those without hope can hope, Walter Benjamin writes, and this is a book about the impossible love between a young, gay man and an aging, sick writer more than twice his age ("the voice I had been inventing for your letters . . . the voice of my life"; the year 1980, the summer of Gdansk, "a Poland to come . . . homeland to us all"; the childhood one can neither keep nor leave; Theodora Katz, "something yet unknown, a new silence of writing; the silence of women, and of the Jews." "My books come from this house," Duras writes. "From this light as well, and from the garden. It has taken me twenty years to write what I just said." One must be where one is, and the longer one is, as Duras surely is, one can speak of it, write it, as few writers can. [Robert Buckeye]

Kate Bernheimer. *The Complete Tales of Merry Gold.* FC2, 2006. 177 pp. Paper: $19.95.

Kate Bernheimer continues her genre-bending saga of the Gold family with *The Complete Tales of Merry Gold*, a sequel to her 2002 novel *The Complete Tales of Ketzia Gold*. Both mine fairytale motifs to tell the Gold sisters' respective stories—Ketzia's poetic and ruminative; Merry's ribald and bleakly comic. Merry grows up despising the more introverted Ketzia, attends fashion school, and ends up a patternmaker for the Children's Clothing Company: "I'm a superior maker of patterns! I've been promoted! This is my gift. Just so. I see forms by day; and by night, I trace pictures from fairy tale books I keep by my bed. This keeps me quiet, this makes me feel whole." But the relief of routine is often short-lived; Merry is haunted by memories of loss. After the death of Semyon, a friend from design school, she sneaks out of his service. "I never returned to my classes," she recalls. "And that is why, to this day, I never make friends. Not a one." Bernheimer's protagonist does not merely parody or appropriate fairy tales. She inhabits them, in the same way that characters in Kafka's anti-parables inhabit parable—clinging to a style and structure that wear thin when tested against life outside the text. When the ill-fitting garment finally tears, Bernheimer exposes truths all the more unsettling for their mock fairy tale innocence. When Merry turns five, she receives a typical assortment of presents—a Baby Alive doll, a toy oven, and a toy sewing kit. Muses the narrator, "Is it really any surprise that, after as many hours as she could stand fake-baking, fake-feeding, and fake-sewing . . . Merry was bored?" Like Steven Millhauser's *Edwin Mullhouse, Merry Gold* evokes childhood and its aftermath in all their often-overlooked complexity. [Pedro Ponce]

Haruki Murakami. *Blind Willow, Sleeping Woman: 24 Stories.* Various trans. Knopf, 2006. 334 pp. $24.95.

To live in a Murakami story is to live at that difficult (albeit enthralling) intersection where explanation gives way to supple mystery, where the everyday reveals layers of disconcerting ambiguity, where motivation becomes irrelevant at that precise moment when it asserts itself most strongly, where tears signal harrowing epiphanies that cannot bear to be spoken, where intimacy suddenly measures distance and vice versa, where clear sight is never the same as insight, where accident implies design and design shatters of its own irony. With the Zen delicacy and hip cool of Raymond Carver (whose stories Murakami has translated) and the fetching eccentricity and skewed comic feel of Kafka, these stories capture with nuance those moments in emotional lives when the heart is stunned by evidence of its own fragility (mirrors are pivotal as are shadowy characters who may or may not be real). Gathered from across more than a decade (most were published originally in *The New Yorker*), these stories, from several translators, maintain their lyric subtleties in their English rendering. A widower interviews for an office assistant willing to wear his dead wife's dresses; a husband on vacation with his wife spends a harrowing night vomiting the worm-ridden food from a romantic dinner; a mother haunts a Hawaiian beach where her son was killed by a shark. These are tales of loneliness, of strangers and chance encounters, unsettling reminders of how an aching heart renders comfort tenuous, how what we gather to our heart invariably lifts and then buries us. Despite Murakami's signature Twilight Zone touches (things and people tend to vanish, animals apparently talk, characters swirl about in dream sequences, and many of the stories hinge on chance meetings and elaborate coincidences), such spectacle effects serve his larger vision of a contemporary world fraught by obscure anxieties and compelled by relationships darkly aware of their own irony. [Joseph Dewey]

Robert Musil. *Posthumous Papers of a Living Author.* Trans. Peter Wortsman. Archipelago Books, 2006. 192 pp. $15.00.

Robert Musil wrote his *Posthumous Papers* during the 1920s for periodicals and newspapers while engaged on *The Man Without Qualities*, his unfinished magnum opus. The stories and feuilletons Musil half-humorously collected in this volume, divided among "Pictures," "Ill-Tempered Observations," "Unstorylike Stories," and one longer tale, "The Blackbird," amply display his considerable range and sophistication in a series of uncanny observations that remain always a step ahead of expectations. The narrator of "Flypaper" takes a fly's-eye view of specimens sinking slowly into exhaustion, struggling within life's snare. Novel perspectives likewise inform the dispassionate scrutiny of primate hierarchies exhibited on "Monkey Island," as well as the folk wisdom of "Can a Horse Laugh?" The respective narrators' self-conscious fascination in "Awakening," "Sarcophagus Cover," and "Slovenian Village Funeral," inspiring introspection before ineffable mysteries, owes much to the curiosity of an author given to intense philosophical speculation. Musil's arch tone in "The Paintspreader," "Binoculars," and "Threatened Oedipus" deflates certain artistic and intellectual fashions of his day, no less subject to absurdity than ours. What might be considered the unaccountable motivations driving the protagonists of "The Giant Agoag," "The Man without Character," and "Children's Story" further suggests a bemused view of human frailty. Finally, in "The Blackbird," Aone and Atwo, men who grew up together but later strayed apart, meet briefly. On this occasion Atwo feels compelled to tell his estranged comrade what life has taught him. As he recounts episodes of love, loss, and regret about his former wife, wartime service, and his mother, in each the figure of a blackbird mimicking a nightingale's song lends a tender, pleading urgency to his, and our, understanding of human existence. These poignant miniatures, arresting in their immediacy and telling details, afford a worthy introduction to a master whose brilliance remains undervalued in English. [Michael Pinker]

Rebecca Goldstein. *Betraying Spinoza: The Renegade Jew Who Gave Us Modernity*. Schocken Books, 2006. 290 pp. $19.95.

Following Robert Pinsky's *The Life of David*, Sherwin B. Nuland's *Maimonides*, and Douglas Century's *Barney Ross*, Rebecca Goldstein's *Betraying Spinoza* is the fourth book in Schocken's "Jewish Encounters" series. Its title defies Spinoza's own austere principles—a champion of absolute reason who was excommunicated from the Jewish community of Amsterdam, he spurned sectarian identities. In her elegant formulation, though, Spinoza is never more Jewish than when challenging the religious category imposed on him in the Europe of the Inquisition and the Reformation, pioneering secularism during an era that did not yet comprehend the term. Goldstein further betrays Spinoza by making her book into a personal encounter, how as an adolescent she fell in love with the philosopher who aspired to a state of radical objectivity, in which the temporal self has been transcended. Both a novelist and a philosopher, Goldstein (whose first novel, *The Mind-Body Problem*, took its title from a persistent ontological conundrum) is ideally equipped for this assignment. She does so by blending memoir, history, philosophy, and biography. Goldstein was taught to mistrust the Jewish heretic and, later, to scorn Spinoza's extravagant presumption about the role of *a priori* reason. However, she discovered an ecstatic quality to Spinoza's thought that she attributed to the historical circumstances of being a Sephardic Jew in Amsterdam. Spinoza sought a solution to the problem of Jewish history in a synoptic vision that transcends both Jewishness and history. Goldstein evokes the poignant image of the pariah Spinoza near the end of his short life returning to visit Amsterdam. He gazes wistfully from a distance at the Jewish community, but his mind is closing in on cosmic truths. Until his death, in a modest rented room, he continues aiming at "an objectivity so radical that even our own demise can be contemplated with equanimity." Though Goldstein presumes to represent Spinoza's thoughts, she respects his goal of objectivity enough not to betray the philosopher with voyeuristic inventions about his life. Nor does she do more than suggest Spinoza's continuing relevance, during a violent time of religious sectarianism and fanatical irrationality. Spinoza moved Albert Einstein (who called him his disciple) to poetry: "Wie liebe ich diesen edlen Mann, mehr als ich mit Worten sagen kann" (How much I love this noble man is more than I can say with words). The words that Goldstein musters explain and sustain such love, even as they acknowledge that biography is an impediment to cosmic understanding. [Steven G. Kellman]

Gerhard Roth. *The Will to Sickness*. Trans. Tristram Wolff. Burning Deck, 2006. 120 pp. Paper: $14.00.

Winter Journey (*Winterreise*) is the title of one Roth novel, and if the title evokes Schubert's song cycle about an unhappy wanderer, it also reflects the landscape the Austrian writer had to traverse in a postwar country still contaminated by Fascism. Somehow one had to start over, shed what was corrupted, give silence a voice. Roth became part of *Forum Stadpark*, which also included Peter Handke and Elfriede Jelinek, a group of writers in Austria, much like *Gruppe 47* in Germany, which not only sought to speak of what Austrians would not acknowledge but also to find new ways of doing so, since the old ways failed. It is no accident that Roth's major seven-volume work, which includes photographs, essays, biography and four novels, is titled *Archive of Silence*. To make himself heard against official silence; to silence it. All his novels are winter journeys of one kind or another, and if this means traveling through a country in which one does not understand the language and nothing is certain, it also means, by necessity, discovering how to address it. "Ornament is a casing," Walter Benjamin notes, and Roth's spare, almost scientific prose strips away ornament. Gone is the controlling voice of the writer who explains, interprets, emphasizes. In *The Will to Sickness* (1973), Roth's third novel, its protagonist, Kalb, sleeps, wakes, eats, walks, talks, shops, eats, walks, visits a prostitute, eats, drinks, sleeps, dreams. Everything is noted as a surveillance camera would record it: minute observation without context, relationship or significance. Kalb also perceives, notes, thinks, but these seem little more than random. ("He collected perceptions like a ragman.") The last sentence of the novel reads, "He believed he recognized the symptoms of sickness in himself, and felt a peculiar satisfaction." Let what is be what is. "No masterpieces," the independent American filmmaker Jack Smith argues. It is the task Roth sets for himself, because it is the only honest one. [Robert Buckeye]

Antonio Tabucchi. *It's Getting Later All the Time*. New Directions, 2006. 232 pp. Paper: $16.00.

The puzzling title of this epistolary novel points the way to my reading. There is a play of words. How can "later" be happening "all the time"? Does "time" have a forward thrust? It does—except for the fact that we *remember* events and people; we are torn between past and future and, to complicate matters, we are in the *present*. Thus time is some mysterious, mythic "structure." Is it any wonder that we never grasp full meaning? We want, for example, to think that the various letters of this novel are sent to *one* woman (except for the final one sent by a mysterious, timeless woman to all the men). If we pause and look closely at passages throughout the novel, we see Tabucchi's artifice: "The past is easier to *read*: one *turns around*, and if possible, takes a look at it. And then, be that as it *may*, the past is always *tangled up somewhere* or other, maybe *even in shreds*" (italics mine). I have emphasized the words that are contradictory or strangely joined. How do we find the "tangle"? Where is it? Does it exist "out there" or in our minds? In fact, we posit an "outside" which exists *inside* our minds. The odd circular moments are emphasized in another letter: "And there is an *indistinct* moment I don't know whether *long or short* (but this doesn't matter much), which the adepts of metempsychosis call the anástole in their *code*, in which everything starts over as the circle *closes and reopens immediately*" (italics mine). We are told by this letter writer (who is he?) that "those who have chosen to enter the circle" don't *know* why they are "there." The moment is compared to "music": "it's like when a piece of music stops and all the instruments *fall short*; that is the moment in which they maintain you come to terms with the lack of *meaning in life*, and so what's the *point of repeating it*? It would be *senseless*" (italics mine). I don't want to suggest that Tabucchi is a grim philosopher; he is, on the contrary, a genial writer who accepts the fact that as much as we cannot capture "what it all means," we must live as fully as we can *now*. And sing!

The novel is jagged and angular, and we are compelled to wait for an answer by "the other"—the woman who seems to be an "oracle." And when we reach the "end" of the novel, we find that she (one of the Fates) cuts "the thread." "Now. At Once. Immediately." The short sentences break through our circular letters, our wishes to "only connect." We give up finding a *solution* to our *yearnings*. We find that, to quote part of a title by the brilliant Americanist John T. Irwin, that there is a "mystery to our solution." We can read this novel many times, and we will remain unsure of all its labyrinthine qualities. And yet we are grateful for our minor misunderstandings, our hallucinatory "illuminations." [Irving Malin]

Toby Olson. *The Bitter Half*. FC2, 2006. 248 pp. $19.95.

Ultimately, Toby Olson is a storyteller, and his stories succeed on the deep relationships his characters have with each other, and the esoteric communities they inhabit. The inherent intimacy of an Olson tale extends to the reader as well, offering a privileged view into singular, often private worlds. The special domains that abound in *The Bitter Half* are various and are strongly defined by class, creating a complex texture that pulls the reader through this compelling tale. The novel's central figure is Pollard, who consults prisons on how to keep their inmates from escaping. Despite being a member of the bourgeoisie, Pollard has forged an intricate relationship with The Kid, an escape artist from a decidedly poor, violent background. Pollard follows The Kid through various unsavory prison systems until being stricken by a particularly dehumanizing but treatable form of cancer. Pollard is forced to recover on a vast estate in rural Wisconsin, and opens up to the reader on multiple levels during this downtime before one last rendezvous with The Kid in the novel's denouement. The "half" in the novel's title refers to the grave events that make up the first half of the 20th century, namely the Great Depression. This backdrop provides an interesting contrast to Pollard's upbringing, who, though monetarily unaffected, cannot shut out the struggling unwashed masses, nor desires to do so. Squatters are graciously accommodated during Pollard's recovery phase, and an affectionate attachment is formed with a roving band of performers, all with freakishly unique talents, something the unconventional Pollard can appreciate. The summarizing of this plot itself reveals problems with its probability, something not helped by some fairly unbelievable coincidences. Such flaws are inherent in Olson's fiction, but they aren't as blatant here as they are in past works like *Seaview*. Despite its blemishes, *The Bitter Half* proves to be an entertaining read because of Olson's ability to spin a yarn. Olson uses the Great Depression as the setting for his story, nothing more, and the odd mix of characters he throws against it makes for a rich, engaging mix, despite the improbability of it all. You'll forget about such misgivings as you get lost in a web of eccentricity, and in Olson's fine prose. [Chris Paddock]

Can Xue. *Blue Light in the Sky & Other Stories*. Trans. Karen Gernant and Chen Zeping. New Directions, 2006. 212 pp. $14.95.

In her Afterword, Can Xue tells us that to access the "realm" of her writing she must first "remove the stone foundation from under [her] feet, and suspend [her] body in a semi-free state," and I believe her. When you enter one of Can Xue's stories, you enter a landscape that, like a dream, is both familiar and otherworldly, the peculiar and the banal combining in such a way as to push everything a little off-balance. So a hole in the floor can ruin a man's life, a little boy will stop talking to scream in your face, and a story's main character might fall asleep just as things get going. Characters fall asleep with curious regularity in these pieces, at inopportune moments, or for inordinate stretches of time; when they wake, it is not always clear (to us or them) that they have woken. In the title story, a girl cuts her foot playing in the yard, then cuts her foot in a dream, then wakes and tries to "go back to the same dream . . . so that she could understand some things better"; in "The Bizarre Wooden Building" the narrator visits an old man who tells him, "I've started to consider how to overcome the obstacle of distance . . . The pitiful child at the door can tell you what the solution is," before falling asleep for the rest of the story. There is something of a blind corner in each of these stories, a Kafkaesque moment when everything becomes something you never expected. Or, rather, there are a series of such moments in every piece, a systematization of the unexpected in which the unexpected is all you can expect. Thus, in Can Xue's work a kind of not-knowing is at stake for reader, characters, and writer as well. "When I write," Can Xue says, "I intentionally erase any knowledge from my mind." If her stories don't traffic in knowledge, they certainly act as occasions for thought. [Danielle Dutton]

Wilhelm Genazino. *The Shoe Tester of Frankfurt*. Trans. Philip Boehm. New Directions, 2006. 132 pp. $14.95.

The German writer, Wilhelm Genazino, asks us to take a walk with him around his native city of Frankfurt in his new novel, *The Shoe Tester of Frankfurt*. Our tour guide is a 46-year-old unnamed narrator who suffers from a massive dose of existential angst because he feels he's living "an unauthorized life." Don't get scared off: this "character's" walk is more like a frolic although it might take him half of Frankfurt to get there. Though our everyman has little to do but walk the streets testing his high-end shoes for a manufacturer, this affords him plenty of time to ruminate and ponder at every block and corner, and over every man and woman, especially women, he passes along the way. And so Genazino has his perennial loser meet with old girl friends and new, have a fling with a hairdresser, survive taking a radical cut in wages from his shoe-testing job only to show up a few blocks farther on at a flea market selling those very same shoes that no longer afford him a livable wage by testing them. Loser, muser, failed lover, outsider, man without ambition, nor a place in the world—in short, all that comprises a life, Genazino plies and piles this narrator's stockpile on with humor and levity, considerable verbal skills and philosophical wit over the course of the journey. By the end of the novel, thanks to a turn at a cocktail party, a twist with a woman, our shoe tester has taken on a new path. No more mere whining and complaining, endless questioning about himself and life—rather he seems finally to have accepted himself and with it, his fate. With a new determination, he is ready for gainful employment, as well as connections with his fellow human beings. [Dick Kalich]

Karen Russell. *St. Lucy's Home for Girls Raised by Wolves*. Knopf, 2006. 242 pp. $22.00.

Russell's first collection of stories amazes me. Most of them, set in a crazy Florida (of the mind?), are so startling in their antic juxtapositions of dream and realism that even their titles are seductive and puzzling. Look, for example, at "Z.Z.'s Sleep-Away Camp for Disordered Dreamers," "Ava Wrestles the Alligator," "Lady Yetil and the Palace of Artificial Snows," and the title story. We must look carefully at them, wondering about "a palace of artificial snows"—what is real snow? What is artificial snow?—and the *nature* of girls raised by wolves. Girls and wolves don't make sense because they belong to different realms. Nature (human, environmental, animal) seems to be out of control—an amazing, transformative marriage of ordinary and extraordinary events, beings, spirits. I want to look closely at the title story: we are given an entry from *The Jesuit Handbook of Lycanthropic Culture Shock*—a book which surely can't exist. Stage one explains: "It is fun for your students to explore their new environment." But the new environment is full of fright. The first sentence follows: "At first, our pack was all hair and snarl and floor-thumping joy." Obviously, something is wrong. We have "hair" and "snarl" instead of ordinary perceptions. Even "joy" is "floor-thumping." What does "thumping" have to do with joy? Wouldn't joy be, on the contrary, airy or ascending? As the story progresses we note that the "girls" are, in effect, animals, using paws, *nosing* "each other midair," "buckling in kinetic laughter." As they near the statue of St. Lucy, they throw their heads back in a "celebratory howl" which is "exultant and terrible." The growing pains, the victory over culture shock, are so suggestive that we don't know where our sympathies lie. Should we admire civilized existence or primitive warfare? Russell is such a fascinating writer because she continually *unbalances* us. The narrator returns home and she is treated as a stranger. The parents stare at her "expectantly . . . waiting for a display of what I had learned." And what has she learned? She has learned to offer a "human lie." And we know that she will never be "at home" with wolves or humans. Nor, by implication, will we. [Irving Malin]

Books Received

Aira, César. *An Episode in the Life of a Landscape Painter*, New Directions, 2006. $12.95. (F)

Alexakis, Vassilis. *Foreign Words*, Autumn Hill Books, 2006. $16.95. (F)

Alsford, Mike. *Heroes & Villains*, Baylor University Press, 2006. $24.95. (NF)

Amis, Martin. *House of Meetings*, Alfred A. Knopf, 2007. $23.00. (F)

Arslan, Antonia. *Skylark Farm*, Alfred A. Knopf, 2007. $23.95. (F)

Barry, Rebecca. *Later, At The Bar*, Simon & Schuster, 2007. $13.00. (F)

Bell, Madison Smartt. *Toussaint Louverture: A Biography*, Pantheon Books, 2007. $27.00. (NF)

Bernstein, Charles. *Girly Man*, University of Chicago Press, 2006. $24.00. (F)

Bock, Dennis. *The Communist's Daughter*, Alfred A. Knopf, 2007. $24.00. (F)

Brady, Taylor. *Occupational Treatment*, Atelos, 2006. $13.50. (F)

Branch, Lori. *Rituals of Spontaneity*, Baylor University Press, 2006. $39.95. (NF)

Brenna, Duff. *The Book of Mamie*, Wordcraft of Oregon, 2006. $18.00. (F)

Brycz, Pavel. *I, City*, Twisted Spoon Press, 2006. $14.50. (F)

Burgin, Richard. *The Conference on Beautiful Moments*, Johns Hopkins University Press, 2007. $18.95. (F)

Campbell, Patty. *Robert Cormier: Daring to Disturb the Universe*, Delacorte Press, 2006. $14.95. (NF)

Choy, Wayson. *All That Matters*, Other Press, 2007. $16.95. (F)

––. *The Jade Peony*, Other Press, 2007. $14.95. (F)

Coffman, Christine E. *Insane Passions: Lesbianism and Psychosis in Literature and Film*, Weslyan University Press, 2006. $49.95. (NF)

Cohen, Joshua. *Cadenza for the Schneidermann Violin Concerto*, Fugue State Press, 2007. $18.00. (F)

Conners, Peter, ed. *PP/FF: An Anthology*, Starcherone Books, 2006. $20.00. (F)

Cowart, David. *Trailing Clouds: Immigrant Fiction in Contemporary America*, Cornell University Press, 2006. $55.00. (NF)

Cupp, Bob. *The Edict*, Alfred A. Knopf, 2007. $24.95. (F)

Danielewski, Mark Z. *Only Revolutions*, Pantheon Books, 2006. $26.00. (F)

Davidson, Craig. *Rust and Bone*, W. W. Norton & Company, 2006. $13.95. (F)

DeCarlo, Montez. *Black Chameleon Memoirs*, Aventine Press, 2006. $12.50. (F)

Di Piero, W. S. *Chinese Apples*, Alfred A. Knopf, 2007. $26.95. (F)

Dills, Todd. *Sons of the Rapture*, Featherproof Books, 2006. $12.95. (F)

Djebar, Assia. *The Tongue's Blood Does Not Run Dry*, Seven Stories Press, 2006. $22.95. (F)

Doppelt, Suzanne. *Ring Rang Wrong*, Burning Deck Press, 2006. $14.00. (F)

Durand, Alain-Phillipe and Naomi Mandel, eds. *Novels of the Contemporary Extreme*, 2006. $110.00. (NF)

Engles, Tim and John N. Duvall, eds. *Approaches to Teaching DeLillo's White Noise*, Modern Language Association of America, 2006. $19.75. (NF)

English, Isobel. *Every Eye*, Black Sparrow Books, 2006. $23.95. (F)

Epstein, Leslie. *The Eighth Wonder of the World*, Handsel Books, 2006. $24.95. (F)

Evaristo, Conceição. *Ponciá Vicencio*, Host Publications, 2007. $20.00. (F)

Farrant, M. A. C. *The Breakdown So Far*, Talon Books, 2007. $17.95. (F)

Fesperman, Dan. *The Prisoner of Guantánamo*, Alfred A. Knopf, 2006. $24.00. (F)

Fowles, John. *The Journals: Volume Two: 1966-1990*, Alfred A. Knopf, 2006. $35.00. (NF)

Fox, Lauren. *Still Life with Husband*, Alfred A. Knopf, 2007. $22.95. (F)

Gaige, Amity. *The Folded World*, Other Press, 2007. $23.95. (F)

Garber, Eugene K. *Vienna ØØ*, Spuyten Duyvil, 2006. $14.95. (F)

Gopnik, Adam. *Through the Children's Gate*, Alfred A. Knopf, 2006. $25.00. (NF)

Gordon, Mary. *The Stories of Mary Gordon*, Pantheon Books, 2006. $26.00. (F)

Greenslit, Sara. *The Blue of Her Body*, Starcherone Books, 2007. $16.00. (F)

Gutkind, Lee and Joanna Clapps Herman, eds. *Our Roots Are Deep With Passion*, Other Press, 2006. $15.95. (NF)

Hall, Oakley. *Warlock*, New York Review of Books, 2006. $16.95. (F)

Harper, Rachel M. *Brass Ankle Blues*, Touchstone, 2006. $13.00. (F)

Harris, Robert. *Imperium*, Simon & Schuster, 2006. $26.00. (F)

Harrison, Jim. *Returning to Earth*, Grove Press, 2007. $24.00. (F)

Heffernan, James A. W. *Cultivating Picturacy: Visual Art and Verbal Interventions*, Baylor University Press, 2006. $44.95. (NF)

Hofmannsthal, Hugo von. *Selected Tales*, Angel Books, 2007. $22.95. (F)

Howard, Joanna. *In the Colorless Round*, Noemi Press, 2006. $10.00. (F)

Howells, William Dean. *The Day of Their Wedding*, Green Integer, 2006. $12.95. (F)

Hubbard, Tom and R. D. S. Jack, eds. *Scotland in Europe*, Rodopi, 2006. $78.00. (NF)

Hunt, Laird. *The Exquisite*, Coffee House Press, 2006. $14.95. (F)

Iannone, A. Pablo. *The Room with Closets*, Vagabond Press, 2006. $10.00. (F)

Irani, Anosh. *The Song of Kahunsha*, Milkweed Editions, 2007. $22.00. (F)

Jaffe, Harold. *Beyond the Techno-Cave*, Starcherone Books, 2007. $16.00. (F)

Jaffe, Harold, ed. *Fiction International 39*, San Diego State University Press, 2006. $12.00. (F)

Johnson, Greg. *Women I've Known*, Ontario Review Press, 2006. $23.95. (F)

Johnson, Jason. *Alina*, Blackstaff Press, 2007. $17.95. (F)

Keller, Tsipi. *Retelling*, Spuyten Duyvil, 2006. $14.00. (F)

King, Martha. *North & South*, Spuyten Duyvil, 2006. $14.00. (F)

Kittredge, William. *The Willow Field*, Alfred A. Knopf, 2006. $24.95. (F)

Klauck, Hans-Josef. *Ancient Letters and the New Testament: A Guide to Context and Exegesis*, Baylor University Press, 2006. $34.95. (NF)

Klowden, Deb and Ben Lerner, eds. *No: a journal of the arts: Issue*

5, No, 2006. $12.00. (F)

Köenings, N. S. *The Blue Taxi*, Little, Brown and Company, 2006. $23.99. (F)

Kohler, Sheila. *Bluebird, or the Invention of Happiness*, Other Press, 2007. $24.95. (F)

Kramer, Frederick Mark. *Apostrophe/Parenthesis*, Journal of Experimental Fiction, 2007. $20.00. (F)

Kramer, Mark and Wendy Call, eds. *Telling True Stories*, Plume, 2007. $15.00. (NF)

Lamothe, Serge. *The Baldwins*, Talonbooks, 2006. $15.95. (F)

Levin, Janna. A Madman Dreams of Turing Machines, Alfred A. Knopf, 2006. $23.95. (F)

Long, Hayley. *Kilburn Hoodoo*, Parthian Books, 2007. $29.95. (F)

Lynch, Brian. *The Winner of Sorrow*, New Island, 2006. $17.64. (F)

Mama, Raouf. *Why Monkeys Live in Trees and Other Stories from Benin*, Curbstone Press, 2006. $12.95. (F)

Mandel, Tom. *To the Cognoscenti*, Atelos, 2007. $13.50. (F)

Maranhas, Mike. *Re'enev*, Pink Granite Productions, 2006. $14.95. (F)

Marías, Javier. *Your Face Tomorrow: Volume Two: Dance and Dream*, New Directions, 2006. $24.95. (F)

Markham, E. A. *At Home with Miss Vanesa*, Tindal Street Press, 2007. $19.95. (F)

Markus, Peter. *Good, Brother*, Calamari Press, 2006. $11.00. (F)

Mason, Daniel. *A Far Country*, Alfred A. Knopf, 2007. $24.00. (F)

Masters, Alexander. *Stuart: A Life Backwards*, Delacorte Press, 2006. $20.00. (NF)

McGuane, Thomas. *Gallatin Canyon*, Alfred A. Knopf, 2006. $24.00. (F)

McMurtry, Larry. *When the Light Goes*, Simon & Schuster, 2007. $24.00. (F)

Meads, Kat. *The Invented Life of Kitty Duncan*, Chiasmus Press, 2006. $14.95. (F)

Mendelson, Edward. *The Things That Matter*, Pantheon Books, 2006. $23.00. (NF)

Miller, Sue, ed. *Best New American Voices 2007*, Harcourt Books, 2006. $14.00. (F)

Montefiore, Santa. *The Gypsy Madonna*, Touchstone Books, 2006. $15.00. (F)

Muñoz, Braulio. *The Peruvian Notebooks*, University of Arizona

Press, 2006. $17.95. (F)

Murakami, Haruki. *After Dark*, Alfred A. Knopf, 2007. $22.00. (F)

Nzewi, Meki. *Okeke: Music, Myth and Life: An African Story*, University of South Africa Press, 2006. $21.69. (F)

Olsen, Lance. *Nietzsche's Kisses*, FC2, 2006. $15.95. (F)

––. *Anxious Pleasures: A Novel After Kafka*, Shoemaker & Hoard, 2007. $15.00. (F)

Osmond, Andrew. *Young British Slacker*, Minnow Press, 2006. $8.99. (F)

Parsa, Amir. *Drive-by Cannibalism in the Baroque Tradition*, Non Serviam Press, 2006. $20.00. (F)

Pate, Gavin. *The Way to Get Here*, Bootstrap Press, 2006. $17.00. (F)

Phelan, Paula. *1919: Misfortune's End*, ZAPmedia, 2007. $14.95. (F)

Pineau, Gisèle. *Devil's Dance*, University of Nebraska Press, 2006. $20.00. (F)

Ping, Wang. *The Last Communist Virgin*, Coffee House Press, 2007. $14.95. (F)

Quintero, Ruben, ed. *A Companion to Satire: Ancient and Modern*, Blackwell Publishing, 2007. $149.95. (NF)

Richter, Stacey. *Twin Study*, Counterpoint, 2007. $23.00. (F)

Samorzewski, Meika Loofs. *Before Country*, Lulu Press, 2007. $11.00. (F)

Savage, Sam. *Firmin: Adventures of a Metropolitan Lowlife*, Coffee House Press, 2006. $14.95. (F)

Smith, Ali. *The Reader*, Constable, 2006. £12.99. (F)

Snyder, Scott. *Voodoo Heart*, Dial Press, 2006. $24.00. (F)

Soseki, Natsume. *The Gate*, Peter Owen, 2006. $23.95. (F)

Sotiropoulos, Ersi. *Zigzag Through the Bitter-Orange Trees*, Interlink Books, 2007. $24.95. (F)

Stavans, Ilan. *The Disappearance*, Northwestern University Press, 2006. $22.95. (F)

Suenaga, Naomi. *The Hundred-Yen Singer*, Peter Owen, 2006. $16.95. (F)

Swann, Stacey, ed. *American Short Fiction: 34*, Badgerdog, 2006. $10.00. (F)

––. *American Short Fiction: 35*, Badgerdog, 2006. $10.00. (F)

Taniguchi, Yuko. *The Ocean in the Closet*, Coffee House Press, 2007. $14.95. (F)

Tatsumi, Takayuki. *Full Metal Apache: Transactions Between Cyberpunk Japan and Avant-Pop America*, Duke University Press, 2006. $22.95. (NF)

Taylor, Marion Ann and Heather E. Weir, eds. *Let Her Speak For Herself*, Baylor University Press, 2006. $44.95. (NF)

Taylor, John. *Paths to Contemporary French Literature: Volume 2*, Transaction Publishers, 2007. $39.95. (NF)

Trewavas, Ed. *Shawnie*, Tindal Street Press, 2006. $15.95. (F)

von der Lippe, Angela. *The Truth About Lou: A {Necessary} Fiction*, Counterpoint, 2007. $24.95. (F)

Walker, Mildred. *The Orange Tree*, University of Nebraska Press, 2006. $12.95. (F)

Walker, Wendy. *Knots*, Aqueduct Press, 2006. $9.00. (F)

Wadi, Farouq. *Homes of the Heart: A Ramallah Chronicle*, Interlink Books, 2007. $12.95. (F)

Washburn, Frances. *Elsie's Business*, University of Nebraska Press, 2006. $17.95. (F)

Wellman, Mac. *Q's Q: An Arboreal Narrative*, Green Integer, 2006. $13.95. (F)

White, Derek. *Poste Restante*, Calamari Press, 2006. $12.00. (F)

Winslow, Don. *The Winter of Frankie Machine*, Alfred A. Knopf, 2006. $24.00. (F)

Yorke, Matthew. *Chancing It*, Waywiser Press, 2006. $13.95. (F)

Zamora, Lois Parkinson. *The Inordinate Eye: New World Baroque and Latin American Fiction*, University of Chicago Press, 2006. $49.00. (NF)

Contributors

PIERRE ALBERT-BIROT was a key figure in France's modernist movement, founding and editing SIC—an early-20th century avant-garde literary magazine—where he helped to shape the work of fellow Futurists, Dadaists, and Surrealists (including Apollinaire, André Breton, Louis Aragon, Philippe Soupault, and the first texts of Tristan Tzara). *The First Book of Grabinoulor* was originally printed in SIC in 1919 but did not appear in English until 1986, translated by Barbara Wright. The first Dalkey Archive edition was published in 2000.

FELIPE ALFAU was born in 1902 in Barcelona. During World War I, he immigrated to the United States, where he studied music and wrote music criticism. In 1936 he published his first novel, *Locos*, for which he was paid $250. His second and final novel, *Chromos*, was written in 1948 and left in a drawer until requested for publication by Dalkey Archive in 1990.

SVETISLAV BASARA, born in 1953, is a major figure in Serbian and Eastern European literature. He is the author of more than twenty literary works, including novels, story collections, and essays. He has received numerous literary awards and his novel *Fuss about Cyclists* (1988) was proclaimed by Serbian literary circles to be one of the ten best novels of the 1980s. Originally published in 1984, *Chinese Letter* was translated by Ana Lucic and published by Dalkey Archive in 2004.

MARC CHOLODENKO is a prolific poet and novelist who has received numerous awards including the Prix Médicis, one of France's highest literary honors. *Mordechai Schamz* was translated into English by Dominic Di Bernardi and published by Dalkey Archive in 1988.

PETER DIMOCK is a former editor at Random House USA, now working at Columbia University Press. *A Short Rhetoric for Leaving the Family* was published by Dalkey Archive in 1998.

WILLIAM EASTLAKE was born in 1917 in Brooklyn to British parents. His mother was confined to a mental institution while he was still an infant, and he and his brother were sent to a boarding school in New Jersey. He worked many jobs across the country and, in 1942, joined the Army. He eventually settled on a ranch in New Mexico, where he befriended the Navajo Indians of the area. He continued to travel and move through the Southwest and elsewhere. He was the author of many novels, including *Bamboo Bed*, *Go in Beauty*, and the trilogy *Lyric of the Circle Heart*. *Castle Keep*, originally published in 1965, was reprinted by Dalkey Archive in 1999.

AIDAN HIGGINS is one of the most highly respected Irish writers of the past fifty years, heir to such master stylists as James Joyce and Samuel Beckett. He is the author of more than a dozen books, including *Langrishe, Go Down*, which won the James Tait Black Memorial Prize and the Irish Academy of Letters Award, and Balcony of Europe, which was shortlisted for the 1972 Booker Prize. *Flotsam & Jetsam*, a collection of selected fiction and prose, was first published in Great Britain in 1996, and in the U.S. by Dalkey Archive Press in 2002. *A Bestiary*, *Windy Arbours*, *Scenes from a Receding Past*, *Bornholm Night-Ferry*, and *Langrishe, Go Down*, are also available from Dalkey Archive.

GERT JONKE is counted among Austria's most important authors and dramatists. He was born in 1946 in Klagenfurt. In 1966, he began studying German literature, history, and music theory at the University of Vienna. After receiving his degree, he worked in the radio play department of South-German Radio in Stuttgart. In 1971, he was a guest of the DAAD artists' program in Berlin and, in the same year, was awarded the Förderungspreis (newcomer award) for literature of the federal land of Carinthia. In following years he spent time in London, Argentina, Hamburg, and Frankfurt. Among other prizes, he has received the Ingeborg-Bachmann Prize, the Erich-Fried Award, and the Great Austria State Prize for literature. Currently, he lives and works in Vienna, Klagenfurt, and Graz. *Geometric Regional Novel* was first published in 1969 and was translated to English in 1994 by Johannes W. Vazulik for Dalkey Archive.

DEBORAH LEVY, a playwright, novelist, and poet, was born in 1959 in South Africa. She moved to Britain with her family and studied theatre at Dartington College of Arts. She was a Creative Arts Fellow at Trinity College, Cambridge, between 1989 and 1991. She is a regular contributor of articles and reviews to newspapers and magazines including *The Independent*, *The Guardian*, and the *New Statesman*. She is also the author of a collection of short stories, *Ophelia and the Great Idea* (1989), and several novels. *An Amorous Discourse in the Suburbs of Hell*, a collection of poems, was published in 1990, and she wrote the screenplay for a short film *Suburban Psycho*, televised by the BBC in 1998. *Billy and Girl* was originally published in England in 1996; Dalkey Archive published the first American edition in 1999. Her latest book is a collection of short stories, *Pillow Talk in Europe and Other Places* (2004), also available from Dalkey Archive.

OSMAN LINS was born in Brazil in 1924. He received many literary prizes, including the Coehlo Neto Prize of the Brazilian Academy of Letters. *The Queen of the Prisons of Greece*, published in Brazil in 1976, was Lins's sixth and final novel and has been praised as the crowning achievement of his career. Dalkey Archive's edition, translated by Adria Frizzi, was published in 1995.

ALF MACLOCHLAINN was born in Dublin in 1926, studied at University College, Dublin, and became a librarian, with internships at the Library of Congress and Simmons College in Boston. He was Director of the National Library of Ireland and Librarian of University College, Galway, chairman of the James Joyce Institute of Ireland, and a trustee of the Chester Beatty Library. He has written film scripts for radio, television, and short films, and has published numerous essays in bibliography, film criticism, and social and intellectual history, as well as satirical verse published in limited editions. *Out of Focus*, first published in Ireland in 1977, was first published in the U.S. by Dalkey Archive in 1985.

WALLACE MARKFIELD, born in 1926, was one of the most important Jewish-American writers of the twentieth century. His novel *To an Early Grave* was adapted into the film *Bye, Bye Braverman*, directed by Sidney Lumet, and he was also the author of *You Could Live If They Let You*, and *Radical Surgery*. First published in 1970,

Teitlebaum's Window was reprinted by Dalkey Archive in 1999.

NICHOLAS MOSLEY was born in London in 1923 and educated at Eton and Oxford. He served in Italy during World War II, and published his first novel, *Spaces of the Dark*, in 1951. Since then, he has published sixteen works of fiction, including the novel *Hopeful Monsters*, winner of the 1990 Whitbread Award. Mosley is also the author of several works of nonfiction, most notably the autobiography *Efforts at Truth* and a biography of his father, Sir Oswald Mosley, *Rules of the Game/Beyond the Pale*. He currently resides in London. *Impossible Object* was first published in 1968, and was reprinted by Dalkey Archive in 1985.

VEDRANA RUDAN was born and still lives in Opatia, Croatia. She lost her job as a radio journalist in the early nineties for satirizing the then-president of Croatia. Currently she writes for *Nacional*, Croatia's biggest and best-selling daily newspaper, and runs a real-estate agency. *Night*, first published in 2002 and translated by Celia Hawkesworth for Dalkey Archive in 2004, has been adapted for the stage as a one-woman monologue and performed in Serbia.

PIOTR SZEWC was born in 1961 in Zamosc, the eastern Polish town that is the model for the town in *Annihilation*. He is currently editor of the periodical Nowe Książki (*New Books*) and his most recent novel, *Bociany Nad Powiatem*, was published in 2005. *Annihilation*, first published in 1987, received widespread critical acclaim and has appeared in English, French, German, and Italian translations. Dalkey Archive published an edition in 1993, translated by Ewa Hryniewicz-Yarbrough.

MATI UNT was an Estonian writer who began his writing career at the age of 19, with a "naïve novel" entitled *Goodbye, Yellow Cat*. From this early beginning, Unt established a broad reputation in the artistic and intellectual circles of Estonia as a writer of fiction, plays, and criticism. His novels *The Debt, On the Existence of Life in Outer Space, Murder in a Hotel*, and *The Autumn Ball*, among others, established Unt as one of the most prolific and well-regarded novelists in Estonia. In addition to his own writing, he was instrumental in bringing avant-garde theater to post-Soviet Union Estonia and was well-known as a director. He died in 2005.

Originally published in Estonian in 1990, *Things in the Night* was translated by Eric Dickens and published by Dalkey Archive in 2006.

DELILLO FIEDLER GASS PYNCHON
University of Delaware Press
Collections on Contemporary Masters

UNDERWORDS
Perspectives on Don
DeLillo's *Underworld*

**Edited by Joseph Dewey, Steven
G. Kellman, and Irving Malin**

Essays by Jackson R. Bryer,
David Cowart, Kathleen
Fitzpatrick, Joanne Gass, Paul
Gleason, Donald J. Greiner,
Robert McMinn, Thomas Myers,
Ira Nadel, Carl Ostrowski,
Timothy L. Parrish, Marc Singer,
and David Yetter

$39.50

LESLIE FIEDLER
AND AMERICAN
CULTURE

**Edited by Steven G. Kellman
and Irving Malin**

Essays by John Barth, Robert
Boyers, James M. Cox, Joseph
Dewey, R.H.W. Dillard, Geoffrey
Green, Irving Feldman, Leslie
Fiedler, Susan Gubar, Jay L.
Halio, Brooke Horvath, David
Ketterer, R.W.B. Lewis, Sanford
Pinsker, Harold Schechter, Daniel
Schwarz, David R. Slavitt, Daniel
Walden, and Mark Royden
Winchell

$36.50

INTO *THE TUNNEL*
Readings of Gass's
Novel

**Edited by Steven G. Kellman
and Irving Malin**

Essays by Rebecca Goldstein,
Donald J. Greiner, Brooke
Horvath, Marcus Klein, Jerome
Klinkowitz, Paul Maliszewski,
James McCourt, Arthur Saltzman,
Susan Stewart, and Heide Ziegler

$35.00

PYNCHON AND
MASON & DIXON

**Edited by Brooke Horvath and
Irving Malin**

Essays by Jeff Baker, Joseph
Dewey, Bernard Duyfhuizen,
David Foreman, Donald J.
Greiner, Brian McHale, Clifford
S. Mead, Arthur Saltzman,
Thomas H. Schaub, David Seed,
and Victor Strandberg

$39.50

ORDER FROM ASSOCIATED UNIVERSITY PRESSES
2010 Eastpark Blvd., Cranbury, New Jersey 08512
PH 609-655-4770   FAX 609-655-8366   E-mail AUP440@ aol.com

NINTH
LETTER

www.ninthletter.com

RECENTLY FEATURING
NEW WRITINGS BY

Oscar Hijuelos

William Wenthe

Lucia Perillo

L.S. Asekoff

Michael Martone

Sheryl St. Germain

Cate Marvin

Ruth Ellen Kocher

Geri Doran

Robin Hemley

Steve Stern

PUBLISHED **SEMI-ANNUALLY** IN **MAY** AND **DECEMBER**

 NINTH LETTER › DEPARTMENT OF ENGLISH › UNIVERSITY OF ILLINOIS
608 S. WRIGHT ST. › URBANA, IL 61801

Bard FICTION PRIZE

Bard College invites submissions for its annual Fiction Prize for young writers.

The Bard Fiction Prize is awarded annually to a promising, emerging writer who is a United States citizen aged 39 years or younger at the time of application. In addition to a monetary award of $30,000, the winner receives an appointment as writer-in-residence at Bard College for one semester without the expectation that he or she teach traditional courses. The recipient will give at least one public lecture and will meet informally with students.

To apply, candidates should write a cover letter describing the project they plan to work on while at Bard and submit a C.V., along with three copies of the published book they feel best represents their work. No manuscripts will be accepted.

Applications for the 2008 prize must be received by July 15, 2007. For further information about the Bard Fiction Prize, call 845-758-7087, send an e-mail to bfp@bard.edu, or visit www.bard.edu/bfp. Applicants may also request information by writing to the Bard Fiction Prize, Bard College, Annandale-on-Hudson, NY 12504-5000.

Bard College PO Box 5000, Annandale-on-Hudson, NY 12504-5000

Dalkey Archive
Scholarly Series

Order any of the following Scholarly Series titles from
WWW.DALKEYARCHIVE.COM before July 30, 2007,
and receive 25% off the cover price

Don't Ever Get Famous:
Essays on New York Writing
after the New York School
DANIEL KANE

Reading Games:
An Aesthetics of Play in
Flann O'Brien, Samuel Beckett, and Georges Perec
KIMBERLY BOHMAN-KALAJA

Rayner Heppenstall:
A Critical Study
G. J. BUCKELL

Fever Vision:
The Life and Works of
Coleman Dowell
EUGENE HAYWORTH

The essays in this book focus attention on the vibrant New York poetry scene of the 1960s and '70s, on the poets who came after what is now known as the New York School. Amiri Baraka, Bernadette Mayer, Hannah Weiner, Clark Coolidge, Anne Waldman, and Ron Padgett are just some of the poets who extended the line that John Ashberry, Frank O'Hara, Kenneth Koch, and James Schuyler started. In *Don't Ever Get Famous*, a range of writers and scholars examine the cultural, sociological, and historical contexts of this wildly diverse group of writers. These poets, many of whom are still writing today, changed American poetry forever, and this book provides the first large-scale consideration of their work.

Don't Ever Get Famous:
Essays on New York Writing after the New York School

DANIEL KANE

Dalkey Archive Scholarly Series
Literary Criticism
$34.95 / paper
ISBN-13: 978-1-56478-460-5
ISBN-10: 1-56478-460-6

"Kane's volume is the first to tackle the period in New York's downtown literary history most closely tied to the group of poets known as the 'Second Generation New York School.' . . . [It] is a must-have for historians of American poetry in the 20th century."

—*Publishers Weekly*

In *Reading Games*, Kimberly Bohman-Kalaja guides us through an entertaining and instructive exploration of a neglected genre of post-modernism, the Play-Text. Pioneered by authors such as Flann O'Brien, Samuel Beckett, and Georges Perec, Bohman-Kalaja's book provides a fresh interpretive approach to understanding the Play-Text. Providing insightful analysis of both game and play theories, and drawing from a wide range of ideas—from the thinking of the great philosophers to basic chess and poker strategies—*Reading Games* makes the world of experimental fiction accessible by unraveling, step-by-step, the innovative strategies of those authors who play reading games.

Reading Games:
An Aesthetics of Play in
Flann O'Brien, Samuel Beckett,
and Georges Perec

KIMBERLY BOHMAN-KALAJA

Dalkey Archive Scholarly Series
Literary Criticism
$34.95 / paper
ISBN-13: 978-1-56478-473-5
ISBN-10: 1-56478-473-8

reading games

An Aesthetics of Play

in Flann O'Brien,

Samuel Beckett,

and Georges Perec

"O'Brien's, Beckett's and Perec's novels are games, irresistibly alluring games. And like any game, in order to play one must begin by learning the rules."

—*Kimberly Bohman-Kalaja*

This book examines the first five novels of Rayner Heppenstall (1911-1981). During his lifetime, many critics cited Heppenstall as the founder of the nouveau roman, believing his debut novel, *The Blaze of Noon* (1939), anticipated the post-war innovations of French writers such as Alain Robbe-Grillet and Nathalie Sarraute. Since his death, however, Heppenstall's reputation has faded, and his fiction is out of print. His final novels, written during a descent into madness, were structurally simplistic and politically unpalatable, and their disastrous critical reception clouded critical judgment of his previous novels. Gareth Buckell examines the importance of technical experimentation, rather than the ideological content, within Heppenstall's earlier works, and seeks a more favorable standing for Heppenstall within our critical and cultural memory.

Rayner Heppenstall:
A Critical Study

G. J. BUCKELL

Dalkey Archive Scholarly Series
Literary Criticism
$29.95 / paper
ISBN-13: 978-1-56478-471-1
ISBN-10: 1-56478-471-1

"Heppenstall's novels were poetic, considered, and intelligently realised engagements with literary form, and, regardless of the sub-discourses of Modernist writing they can justifiably be situated within, they deserve a far better reputation."

—G. J. Buckell

From his birth in rural Kentucky during the Great Depression to his suicide in Manhattan in 1985, Coleman Dowell played many roles. He was a songwriter and lyricist for television. He was a model. He was a Broadway playwright. He served in the U.S. Army, both abroad and at home. And most notably, he was the author of novels that Edmund White, among others, has called "masterpieces." But Dowell was deeply troubled by a deperssion that hung over him his entire life. Pegged as both a Southern writer and a gay writer, he loathed such categorization, preferring to be judged only by his work. *Fever Vision* describes one of the most tormented, talented, and inventive writers of recent American literature, and shows how his eventful life contributed to the making of his incredible art.

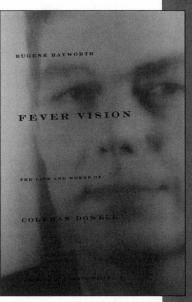

Fever Vision:
The Life and Works of
Coleman Dowell

EUGENE HAYWORTH

Dalkey Archive Scholarly Series
A Biography
$24.95 / paper
ISBN: 1-56478-457-6

"Gene Hayworth has done his homework by interviewing surviving family members and friends and by reading early drafts and letters and everything unpublished that the estate has made available. . . . This is a cautionary tale, perhaps— though what it mainly seems to be cautioning us against is a sentiment that overtakes most people with time: disappointment."

—*Edmund White,*
from the Introduction

ORDER FORM

Individuals may use this form to subscribe to the *Review of Contemporary Fiction* or to order back issues of the *Review* and Dalkey Archive titles at a discount (see below for details).

Title	ISBN	Quantity	Price

Subtotal _____

Less Discount _____
(10% for one book, 20% for two or more books)

Subtotal _____

Plus Postage _____
(domestic: $3 + $1 per book / foreign: $5 + $3 per book)

1 Year Individual Subscription to the **Review** _____
($17 domestic, $20.50 foreign)

Total _____

Mailing Address _____

_____

_____

_____

xxvi/3

Credit card payment ☐ Visa ☐ Mastercard

Acct. # _____ Exp. Date _____

Name on card _____ Phone # _____

Please make checks (in U.S. dollars only) payable to *Dalkey Archive Press*

mail or fax this form to: Dalkey Archive Press, University of Illinois, 605 E. Springfield, MC-475, Champaign, IL 61820
fax: 217.244.9142; *tel:* 217.244.5700